GARDEN SENSE

Secrets of an
Experienced Gardener

ROY JONSSON

*To Renee & Jim
Happy Gardening
Roy Jonsson*

For more information contact:
www.royjonsson.com
roy_jonsson@telus.net

LIBRARY AND ARCHIVES CANADA CATALOGING IN PUBLICATION

Jonsson, Roy
  Garden sense / Roy Jonsson.

Includes index.
ISBN 978-0-9782884-0-2

  1. Gardening. i. Title.

SB453.J67 2007   635   C2007-900980-8

Cover photo by Sue Dawson
Photos and line drawings by Roy Jonsson
Design and layout by Vancouver Desktop Publishing Centre
(www.self-publish.ca)
Printed in Canada by Impress Digital (www.impressdigital.com)

This book is dedicated to Margaret—wife, editor and critic—who has accompanied me on many garden tours and horticultural trips and shares my love of plants.

Contents

What Other Garden Books Don't Tell You

After working in the world of gardening and landscaping for more than twenty-five years I came to the conclusion there are very few books that really help both beginning and experienced gardeners fully understand the wonderful world of horticulture. As a horticultural instructor, consultant and garden columnist I have had to do extensive research on a wide variety of plant-related topics over the years. Even though I have hundreds of garden books and a large filing cabinet bursting with files, I'm often unable to find the information I need. My garden students, clients and readers often ask questions about terminology, garden practices, planting procedures and growth patterns that most garden books skim over or do not cover at all.

In this book I have not attempted to cover everything in the field of horticulture but will share with you what I have learned over many years, some of the secrets that every gardener needs to know to create and maintain a great garden.

CHAPTER ONE

Soil

The Foundation of All Gardens

As one writer said "Create a healthy soil and you will have the potential to build a healthy and productive garden."

Physical Composition

Native or naturally-occurring soils consist of four different particles based on size. Each of the four particles has distinct characteristics and their presence helps classify the soil type.

- **Clay:** The smallest particle in soil (less than .005 mm) is deposited most often by water and tends to be very sticky when wet. Clay particles form plate-like structures and become impermeable to water, air, roots and, if highly compacted, even earthworms. To prevent damage to the soil structure, gardeners should not walk on or try to work very wet clay soils. A sample of very wet clay soil rubbed between your thumb and index finger should feel slippery, sticky or greasy. A wet clay soil sample can also be rolled into a long worm-like form.

- **Silt:** Also generally deposited by water, this is the second largest particle (.002 mm to .05 mm) found in soil. Silt often is mistaken for clay and smaller silt particles can have the same characteristics as clay. When tested, silt will feel slightly gritty when rubbed between the fingers. Most great river deltas are a mix of clay and silt soil that support some of the world's most intensive agriculture and densely-populated areas.

- **Sand:** The third largest particle (.001 mm to .078 mm) will not pack as tightly as silt or clay. Air and water tends to pass through sand much more readily. When rubbed between the fingers, sand will feel very gritty.

- **Gravel and Rocks:** Often part of the soil, but these are not one of the main components. Gravel (2 mm to 7.5 mm) and rocks (larger than 7.5 mm) are not beneficial to soil in most cases and can make the soil unusable in some instances.

Four components of a typical soil

The physical properties of soil can have an effect on water-holding capacity, aeration, drainage, ease of tillage, root growth and fertility.

Soil can be analysed and named by examining its physical composition and particle size. Soils that contain a single-sized soil particle are classified as either clay, silt or sand. When two or more of these particle sizes are mixed together, the soil is then referred to as a loam and named by the predominate particle, i.e. clay loam, silt loam or sandy loam. Some of the best soil contains all three particle sizes. Although organic content is not used to

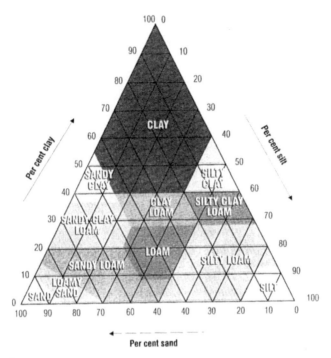

Soil graph.

classify soil, some soils with a very high organic content (30%+) are referred to as muck or peat soils. Each combination or mix of soil particles creates a different soil with unique properties. Knowing the garden's soil properties helps the gardener better manage the soil and choose the right plants.

There are several simple tests that a gardener can perform to help determine soil texture.

- **Graininess Test:** Rub a small sample of soil between your fingers. If the soil contains sand it will feel grainy or gritty.

- **Moist Cast Test:** Squeeze a sample of soil in your hand to form a cast and then relax your fingers to see if the cast holds together. When tossed from hand to hand the more durable the cast, the higher the clay content.

- **Stickiness Test:** Squeeze a sample of wet soil between your thumb and forefinger and check to see the level of stickiness when the pressure is released. The greater the stickiness the greater the clay content.

- **Worm Test:** Roll a soil sample in the palm of your hand to form a long worm. The more clay present, the longer and thinner the worm will be before breaking.

The structure of soil, or arrangement of soil particles, determines pore space, which can vary from 20% to 50% of soil volume. Pore space will determine the rate at which gases such as oxygen, carbon dioxide and nitrogen can move in or out of the soil, all of which can affect root growth, earthworm activity and micro-organisms. Roots in non-porous or poorly drained soil will not receive the air they need to grow and develop.

To test for drainage, dig a hole 15 cm wide and 30 cm deep, and fill it with water. When the hole has drained refill it and keep track of the time it takes to drain a second time. If it takes more than four hours, you have a drainage problem.

A similar test for earthworm activity can be done by removing a 30 cm cube from a soil area that has at least 25% moisture, has not been dug over recently and is at least 12°C (55°F). Sieve the soil and count the earthworms. Ten worms is the equivalent to 500,000/acre, so the soil is in good shape. Fewer than five worms may indicate the soil is lacking in biological activity due to a lack of organic matter, compaction or an imbalance in the pH. (*See page 17 for correcting pH imbalance.*)

Soil Amendments

Few soils have an ideal soil structure. However, soil structure can be modified by adding amendments. Organic matter such as compost is the most common material added to clay, silt and

sandy soils. It will help to correct most of the negative characteristics of all three soils. Other amendments that are commonly
used are manure and mushroom compost. Some amendments
are superior to others, depending on the characteristics the gardener wants to achieve. Potting soils and greenhouse media may
have other amendments added to create specific qualities.

Soil Amendment Properties

Amendment	Bulk Density (g/ccm)	pH	CEC*	Fertility
Compost	6.5 - 7.0	high	high	high
Diatommite	7	7	low	low
Peat	4.5 - 7.0	high	low	low
Perlite	0.10 - 0.14	7 - 7.5	low	very low
Pumice	0.09 - 0.20	7 - 7.4	low	very low
Sand	1.45 - 1.70	4.5 - 8.5	low	very low

* Cation Exchange Capacity is the ability of soil to hold nutrients by electrical
  charges.

Soil Colour

The colour of the soil reflects the parent material or amendments
that have been added by nature or human activity. For example,
weathered limestone will form into a gray clay, soils rich in iron
and aluminum are brick red. Most gardeners associate black soils
with fertility, which is generally true. The darkness of the soil is
generally related to the organic content, the amount of carbon
deposited in the soil and the effect of humic acid. Many of the wet
grasslands of the world have very black soils that formed after
the last glaciation period some 10,000 years ago. Year after year
the dead grass built up the organic and carbon content in the soil
to produce a very rich black loam. The dark colour of soil will
help absorb more solar radiation, warm more quickly and produce an earlier crop.

Soil pH

Most gardeners know the pH scale is used to measure acidity and alkalinity but many do not know what pH means or how the calibration on the scale works. pH stands for potential hydrogen ions, and is also referred to as "soil reaction" or the concentration of hydrogen ions (H+) and hydroxyl ions (OH-) in a soil solution. Basic or alkaline soils have a concentration of (OH-) ions and acidic soils have a concentration of (H+) ions. The pH scale runs from 0 to 14 with 7 being neutral. If there is a greater concentration of (H+)

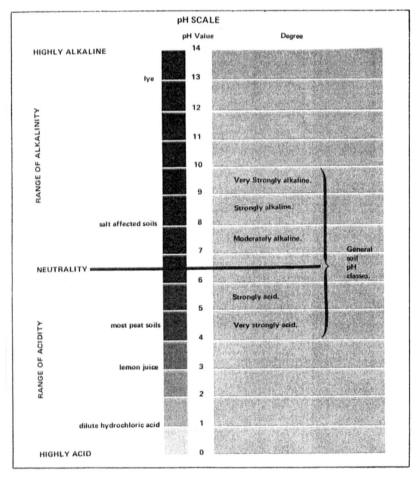

Ph scale.

ions then the reading will be below 7, or acidic. If the (OH-) ions are more numerous, then the reading will be above 7, or alkaline. Unlike a regular ruler with an arithmetic scale, the pH scale is a logarithmic scale where each number is ten times larger than the previous one. Hence a reading of 6 is ten times more than 5, and 7 is a hundred times more than 5.

Soils in high rainfall regions gradually become more acidic while those in arid regions become more alkaline over time. Most rain water has some natural carbon dioxide dissolved in it. This forms a weak solution of carbonic acid. With the increase in industrial pollution, there is more acid rain in many areas that will also affect the pH of soil.

Soils in arid regions with low rainfall and high rates of evaporation leave behind concentrations of calcium, magnesium, potassium and other alkaline salts. This is particularly noticeable around the shores of alkaline lakes in arid and semi-arid regions. Certain horticultural practices, such as using sulphate, phosphate and nitrate-based fertilizers, can also lower the natural pH of the soil.

Plant life has a wide range of tolerance for levels of acidic and alkaline soils. Some bog plants can tolerate pH levels of 4.5 or less, whereas cactus and salt brush survive at 8.5. The most productive

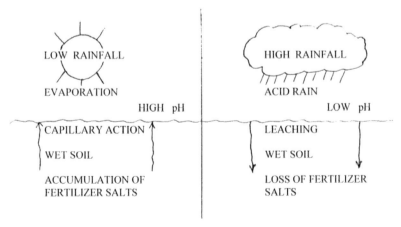

Acid and alkaline conditions in high and low rainfall areas.

agricultural soils are in the 6.5 to 7.5 range. However there is a group of plants that are known as acid lovers, preferring a pH of approximately 5.5. Azaleas, camellias, heather, pieris, rhododendrons and blueberries are just a few examples. Most ericaceous plants prefer an acid type soil.

Each plant will have its own level of tolerance, but many plants seem to be more comfortable at 6.5 than any other reading.

Placing plants outside their natural pH tolerance level will cause them to perform poorly for a variety of reasons: they may lack one or more plant nutrients or the plant nutrients may not be in a form that is available to them, beneficial soil microbes may not be active or toxic ions may be harmful to the plants. As plants grow, they can alter the pH of the substrate close to the root system. In greenhouse trials, it was found that geraniums will lower the pH and zinnias will raise the pH of the soils in which they are planted.

Historically, horticulturalists referred to acidic soils as sour soils because most acidic things are sour to the taste. They would then add lime to sweeten the soil, or raise the pH. The term "sweeten" is opposite to sour, but is technically incorrect because alkaline substances are bitter not sweet.

Some flowers such as Hydrangea macrophylla can act as a natural litmus paper. As the soil becomes more acidic the flowers turn a deeper blue, and as the soil becomes more alkaline the flowers become a deeper pink colour. Placing lime on one side of the plant and aluminum sulphate on the other side will create both pink and blue flowers on the same plant.

Adjusting Soil pH

In regions of high precipitation such as the Pacific Northwest where soils become too acidic, the pH can be adjusted by adding calcium and/or magnesium in any one of the following forms:

- **Dolomite Limestone**: Normal limestone consists of calcium carbonate whereas dolomite contains both calcium and magnesium carbonate, both of which are plant nutrients. In areas where soils are rich in magnesium, it is better to use calcium carbonate. This crushed dolomite limestone rock comes as coarse (sugar consistency), fine (flour consistency) or prilled (powder formed into pellets). As can be expected, the coarse product is slower to release than the fine, and it lasts longer. The prilled material is very fine, and is prilled for ease of application. When added to soil, even the finest dolomite will take a month or more to have any appreciable effect on the soil's pH. There is no danger of burning grass or plant roots with dolomite lime. Apply at a rate of 20 kg/97m^2 or 44 lbs/1000ft^2.

- **Agricultural Lime** (Slaked Lime): This product is no longer a popular soil amendment because, although it is quick acting, it has a tendency to burn root hairs when applied. It is also caustic to eyes and open cuts. When limestone is burned in a lime kiln it produces calcium oxide (quick lime) which is converted into calcium hydroxide by adding water. The calcium hydroxide, a strong alkaline substance, is then dried and sold as agricultural lime.

In regions of low precipitation where the soil pH is too high, the soil can be amended with one of the following:
- elemental sulphur,
- aluminum sulphate,
- sulphate, phosphate, or nitrate based fertilizers.

Which product to use will depend on the size and nature of the planting and how quickly you want to adjust the pH. Commercially available aluminum sulphate is the best product for spot treatments of specific acid-loving plants. Apply at a rate of 5 to 20 kg/97m^2 or 10 to 40 lbs/1000 sq. ft.

Making a small change to the soil pH by adding dolomite (to make more alkaline) or aluminum sulphate (to make more acidic) is a relatively simple matter. Making a large change over a short time is virtually impossible. If it takes 20 kgs of dolomite lime to raise the pH from 5.5 to 6 on a 100 m² lawn, then it will require 200 kgs of lime to raise it to 6.5, and 2000 kg to raise it to 7. At a rate of 20 kg the lime is slightly visible on the grass, at 200 kg the grass will be white and at 2000 kg it will be up to your ankles. Adding lime twice per year in high rainfall areas (spring and fall) in the first year will help speed the process. Soil sulphur and liming materials are not highly soluble and therefore are effective only as deeply as they are incorporated. (*For Soil Testing, see Chapter 3: Fertilizers.*)

Soil Microbial Life: Bacteria and Fungi

For years soil scientists and gardeners assumed that all plants needed for good growth was soil, water and fertilizer. They have now come to understand there is much more to soil biology. Soil biology is as important as soil chemistry. A healthy soil is now defined as one that has the right set of both nutrients and soil organisms required for the desired type of plant growth. Beneficial soil organisms come in the form of worms, bacteria, fungi, protozoa, nematodes, mycorrhizal fungi and micro-arthropods. To function properly in soil, microbes need an aerobic atmosphere, a relatively neutral pH and adequate food to grow and multiply.

Microbes in the soil play an important role in plant establishment, survival and succession. Each form of vegetation performs best when it has the proper ratio of fungus to bacteria in the soil.

Young soils tend to be compacted and are first colonized by weeds where the ratio of fungus to bacteria is (.1:1) and then by simple grasses (.3:1), more complex grasses (.75:1), row crops (1:1), shrubs and vines (2-5:1), deciduous trees (5-100:1) and coniferous trees (100-1000:1). Any natural disturbance, such as overgrazing, fire, flood or volcanic activity, will push the system back towards the youthful soil character and weed-like vegetation. When applying this concept to orchards, one should have woody shrubs, not an understory of grass, to help raise the fungal ratio. Too much tillage, excess fertilizer and the use of pesticides are three things that harm microbial activity.

Tillage, particularly with larger woody shrubs and trees, breaks up the strands of mycelium formed by beneficial fungus and reduces their effectiveness in controlling pathogens and in developing a symbiotic relationship with the plant roots. In general, the larger the tree (particularly conifers) the greater the mass of beneficial fungus in and around the root system.

Highly compacted soils can be a major problem for most plants. Compacted soils have very little oxygen and quickly become anaerobic, a condition that encourages harmful pathogens and the production of lethal alcohol. Compacted soils rich in NO_3, such as lawns, will cause grass roots to die. This is why golf courses aerate their greens and fairways so frequently during the golfing season. The length of grass roots has less to do with blade length and more to do with compaction and the supply of oxygen. Beneficial fungi need oxygen to survive and in turn will help to hold calcium in the soil, preventing acidification.

When applying a chemical fertilizer, gardeners tend to forget they are adding a strong salt to the living area of millions of beneficial microbes. As the fertilizer granules dissolve in the soil moisture, the strong salt solution often kills the microbes due to osmotic shock. In other words, the protoplasm in the microbe's body is pulled out through the cell wall into the more dense salt solution, causing the cells to collapse and the microbe to die. It is ironic that the fertilizer salts kill the very bacteria that are often required to convert ammonium nitrogen into nitrate nitrogen so the plants can use it.

Having a high level of bacterial life in the soil helps to build soil structure because the bacteria will glue together microscopic soil particles or colloids, which are like building bricks. With good soil structure there is more oxygen, better drainage, more earthworm activity and less trapped gases in the soil. Most pesticides, both insecticides and fungicides, are designed to kill harmful bacteria and fungus and are generally non-selective. Used on plants or in the soil, they can do great harm to the beneficial microbial life in the soil.

Mycorrhizal fungus plays an extremely important role in the life and health of plants. The fungus forms in and around the plants roots and enters into a symbiotic relationship with the plants. There are two general groups of mycorrhizal fungus. Ectomycorrhizae, modifies the exterior of the root as part of the relationship and endomycorrhizae modifies only the internal structure of the root. This fungus has the ability to supply plants with basic nutrients and in return absorbs sugars, carbohydrates and proteins produced by the plant. The fungus is able to increase the absorbing surface area of the root from 10 to 1000 times, thereby making the plant far more efficient at taking up nutrients. Another benefit is the mycorrhizae ability to release powerful chemicals into the soil to dissolve those hard-to-access nutrients such as iron and phosphate. Mycorrhizal fungus will attack pathogens and prevent disease from entering the roots. Three common diseases that are held in check by mycorrizae fungus are Phytophthora, Fusarium and Rhizoctonia. Mycorrhizal fungus also assists plants during drought conditions by helping them take up water. The fungus-root coexistence is mutually beneficial and necessary for optimal growth. As mentioned before, the amount of mycorrhizal fungus increases as forests mature and is most plentiful in old growth coniferous forests.

Commercial Topsoil

In most jurisdictions it is against the law to scrape topsoil from agricultural or crown land and sell it to homeowners or commercial landscapers. Virtually all topsoil is a manufactured product that is made from three resources and a variety of amendments.

- **Reclaimed Soil:** Topsoil, subsoil and hardpan that is removed from construction sites is taken to a soil manufacturer where the material is screened and amended to produce a low-grade topsoil. This soil often has a high clay content, is low in nutrients and may be contaminated with noxious weeds, such as horsetail and morningglory, weed seeds or industrial waste. Instead of a truckload of soil you may be getting a truckload of trouble.

- **Peat Soil:** Sedge peat deposits are removed from construction sites or from peat bogs and used to produce commercial topsoil. The peat is high in organic matter but low in nutrients and will absorb and hold excess moisture in high rainfall areas. Most peat has a very low pH. It is frequently used for amending other types of topsoil.

- **Compost-Based Soil:** Many municipalities and some private companies collect green waste at local transfer stations and produce commercial compost. High heat sterilizes the compost and kills weeds, weed seeds and pathogens. It is rich in nutrients with a pH of 7 or slightly higher. Most compost-based soils are blended with sand and peat, have a high organic content and will hold excess moisture in wet climates.

Commercial Topsoil Amendments

Each commercial topsoil will contain a variety of different amendments depending on availability and the quality of the end product desired. The most common amendments are sand, sedge peat, steer manure, mushroom compost, commercial compost, composted bark and tertiary treated sewage sludge. Less common and less beneficial are horse manure (see section on Animal Manures.), raw sawdust and ground bark. For topping up beds and soil renewal where organic material has been depleted, it is better to use commercial compost or steer manure and amend the soil you have, rather than purchase more sand, clay or peat as topsoil. Perlite or pumice are often used to create lightweight, well drained potting soils for containers, rooftop gardens or greenhouse use. Some books recommend the use of sand to modify heavy clay soils but this can lead to serious problems. In the right proportions, clay can act as cement and sand as the aggregate and together they may harden into something similar to concrete. Organic matter such as compost, manure or peat is a far better soil conditioner than sand, in most cases. Books from England often refer to potting soil as compost whereas in North America we generally reserve that word for decayed organic material.

CHAPTER TWO

Compost

Nature's Own Fertilizer

Mother Nature has been producing compost from dead and decaying organic material (humus) since the beginning of time. A good functioning compost box speeds up the natural process and protects the nutrients from being leached before the compost is added to the garden. For best results, a compost pile should have the right balance or ratio of green materials (high nitrogen) to brown materials (high carbon), preferably well mixed or laid down in layers.

A good ratio of carbon (brown) to nitrogen (green) is approximately 25:1 although it is impossible to accurately measure this ratio without using a lab test. Mixing equal quantities of green material to brown material will be a good guide to get started and then it becomes a game of trial and error until the right balance is achieved with experience. As with soil, a good quality compost has to be made under aerobic conditions. Poking holes in the compost on a regular basis or turning the pile allows the beneficial microbes to get the oxygen they need. Under the right conditions the microbes will multiply at a phenomenal rate.

A compost pile needs heat to work. The pile will go through three stages of heating depending on the type of bacteria that is active. The first stage called psychrophilic generally functions between 0° and 18° with the optimum being 13°C. The second or mesophilic stage is between 4° and 43°C with the optimum being 27°C. The third is the thermophilic stage, which operates best between 40° and 93°C with an optimum of 66°C. Most of the breakdown occurs in the mesophilic stage but the weed seeds and pathogens are not killed until the pile reaches the upper thermophilic stage. Adding small amounts of debris to the pile on a regular basis will rarely cause the pile to heat and reach the thermophilic stage – it is best to stockpile material and then add a large amount of material at one time to achieve the necessary heating. The temperature of the pile is a good indicator of the microbial activity and the speed at which the pile is breaking down into plant food. The heat should be greater than 57°C (135°F) but less than 71°C (160°F) for more than three days to kill the pathogens but not harm the beneficial bacteria.

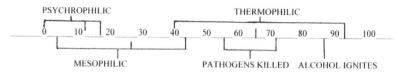

Temperature limits and activity.

Earthworms play an important role in compost piles by digesting humus material and producing their own body weight in worm castings (manure) each day, providing food for the microbes in the pile. The tunnels they make in the pile form passages for gas exchange. Earthworms start laying eggs after three or four months and have the ability, under the right conditions, to increase their numbers exponentially. Earthworms are like birds in that they have a gizzard and need grit to grind up their organic food. Adding a scoop of new or recycled soil to the compost pile every week or two will keep the earthworms from leaving their job in the compost pile and going in search of grit. However, a thick layer of soil will smother the pile and stop the flow of oxygen.

Humic acid will form as organic debris breaks down, causing the compost to turn brown. This helps to explain why peat and water from peat bogs are a deep brown colour. The greater the breakdown, the darker the material. Colour can then become an indicator of soil fertility.

If the interior of the compost pile does not get enough oxygen and turns anaerobic, the wrong microbes become dominant and pathogens can survive. The bi-products from an anaerobic pile are not carbon dioxide and water but alcohol, hydrogen sulphide (rotten eggs), phosphene gas (swamp gas), acetic acid, butteric acid and volaric acid (vomit). No wonder a poorly managed compost pile is inclined to stink! Much of the useful ammonia (NH_3) is lost to the atmosphere and the compost will have a very low pH. Alcohol produced will also boil off and ignite at 88°C (190°F), a major cause of fires in compost piles and hay barns.

Adding lime to a compost pile will combine with ammonium cations to form ammonia gas that is then lost to the atmosphere. The addition of phosphate will absorb ammonia and become a nutrient.

Compost can be added to soil in a variety of ways. Mulching is the most common way but it can also be added by pulling plugs from a lawn and adding compost into the core holes, by incorporating compost in newly tilled soil, or by adding compost as an amendment to potting soil. The use of too much compost for repotting houseplants will sometimes attract fungus gnats (little black flies).

With new compost "soup" or "tea" machines being marketed, it is now possible to spray liquid compost on plants to feed them. This helps to deter many fungal diseases. For example compost tea will prevent the lawn fungus Red Thread from infecting grass. To make a good compost tea you will need both bacterial and fungal food. Common ingredients are kelp (a good sticker), rock dust, fish concentrate, molasses, fruit juice, plant extracts and a constant supply of oxygen supplied with an air pump. Coating the leaves with compost tea helps to smother fungal diseases.

Compost Boxes or Bins

The ideal size for a home compost box is between a cubic yard (3 ft x 3 ft x 3 ft) and a cubic metre. A smaller box is unlikely to generate very much heat and a larger box may not be able to get rid of the waste carbon dioxide gas or draw in enough oxygen to support the bacteria. Two or three boxes of this size are better than one big one. This allows the home gardener to let the contents of one box mature while filling the other ones.

Where to place a compost box is important. It must be in an area that is readily accessible for a wheelbarrow to haul refuse to it and finished compost away from it. A sunny area may increase the temperature of the box slightly but I like to keep those areas for growing. A shady site in the garden that can be screened off would be a good spot for a compost box, pots, stakes and surplus soil. The ground should be level, well drained and not close to any noxious weeds, such as morningglory, that can invade the rich source of nutrients.

A warning: compost mixed with sections of root from plants such as morningglory will contaminate your entire garden.

Suitable Materials for Compost

There is a wide range of suitable material that can be added to a compost box. Any garden waste or leaves that are not woody or leathery in nature are good. All vegetable kitchen waste, including tea bags, coffee grounds (and filters), is excellent. Disregard the myths about not putting rhubarb leaves, grapefruit rinds, cereals and cooked vegetable matter in the compost—these are fine. Lawn clippings are high in nitrogen (approximately 4%) and are best mixed with an equal amount of brown material and limited to 10 to 20 cm layers. (Large volumes of lawn clippings will heat rapidly and then turn into a grey slimy mat that may turn the pile anaerobic.) Modest layers of manures can be added to the pile if you are short of nitrogen-rich materials or if you want to increase the nutrient level of the compost. Freshly

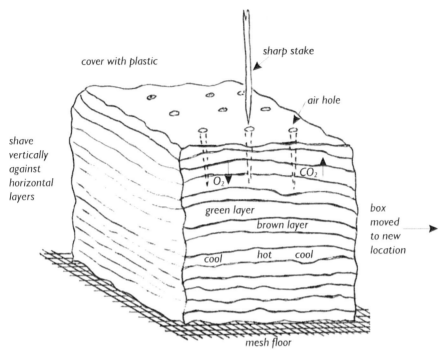

Cross section of compost pile

collected seaweed is another excellent supplement. Do not try to store or stockpile seaweed in plastic bags for later use as it will turn into a slimy mess. Gardeners who make wine or beer can add the waste to the compost in modest layers, providing it is well oxygenated. The production of alcohol will kill the beneficial bacteria. A fine film of wood ash on the surface to keep the flies under control may be useful but remember that wet ash produces a caustic lye solution that can kill the beneficial bacteria in the pile.

Not Suitable for Compost

Things that are not suitable for a compost pile are not as easily defined. Avoid all pet feces except that of chickens, rabbits and ducks. Dog and cat feces have too much fat, protein and hair to break down. Both types of feces may have pathogens that can be transferred to humans. Infected plants such as Club Root in brassica crops can remain in the soil for several years. All fats, oils, meat and bones are not easily broken down by bacteria.

Weeds make good compost, providing they have not gone to seed or are prone to grow from small sections of root. It is best to send them out with the garbage, crush roots (rather than cut them), or heat them in the sunlight in a clear plastic bag for a few days until they will not grow again. Then add them to the compost pile.

Hard or leathery leaves, such as laurel or rhododendron, will not break down in a compost pile. Oak leaves will decay but it will take two years. Evergreen fern fronds and lawn moss will not break down at all. Eggshells are a minor source of calcium but they also take several years to disintegrate. When shells are added to the garden, the bed will look as if it has been covered with confetti.

A well-managed compost box must have the right mix of materials, sufficient moisture (about the same as a wrung-out sponge) and plenty of oxygen. Turning over and mixing up the contents of a full compost box three times during a six week period will produce some good compost in a short time, but it requires a great deal of hard work. I prefer to aerate my pile with a large sharp stick as I add material over the course of a growing season and into the winter. For a square metre surface I poke about 10 to 12 holes as deep as the sharp stick will go. This creates a passage for the oxygen to enter the pile and the carbon dioxide to escape. The temperature of the stick's surface when removed will also give an indication if the pile is heating or not. Some compost guides suggest you place woody branches in the pile to help aerate the material but this will create a messy tangle when you empty the compost.

During the fall when the leaves are coming down I rake them up and store them dry in large plastic pallet bags to put into the compost pile gradually over the winter when I have nothing to mix with sloppy, wet kitchen waste. An alternative is to dig a shallow hole in the top of the compost pile and dump your kitchen waste in the hole and them pull some of the rough material back on top. This is similar to running a worm bin in the compost pile. Just remember that the material in this "worm bin" will be much richer than the rest of the compost and may benefit from blending with the regular compost. (*See the section below on Worm Bins for more details.*)

In late February or early March, remove a layer of fresh material from the top of the pile and place it in a second box as a base or starter for a new pile and use the fully decayed compost below. Be sure to slice the finished compost in a vertical fashion, which is the opposite direction to the horizontal layers added to the box.

Creating good compost can be a challenge for a beginning gardener unless you follow the basic rules. Here are a few things to check if the pile does not seem to be functioning properly:

- **The compost pile or fresh compost smells**: There is too little air. Poke deep holes in the pile or turn the compost.

- **The compost pile dries out:** Take the cover off and let in some rain water or spray water on the pile.

- **The compost pile is slow to decay**: Check for lack of oxygen, lack of water or too much water, wrong ratio of nitrogen to carbon, or material that is too woody and will not break down.

Garden Box Composting System

inside dimension:
3' x 3'

Parts List
- 12 3' – 2 x 2
- 20 3' – 1 x 6
- 4 3' – 1 x 3
- 4 3' – 1 x 2
- 12 screws
- 21' 19 g. 1/2" wire mesh

mesh on frame

LID ASSEMBLY

1 x 3

2 x 2

1 x 2

Choosing a Site

Select a suitable site for your compost box:
- easily accessible
- on level surface (soil or grass)
- in sun or shade
- well drained
- at least 4' x 7' in area
- free of pernicious weeds, e.g. morningglory
- preferably out of view or screened with hedge or plantings

Be sure the position of your box allows access for later removal of the front panel and allows room to slide the box away from the pile of ready-to-use compost next spring.

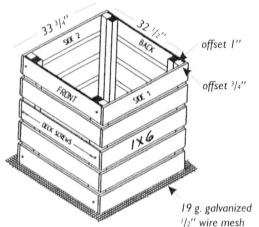

offset 1"

offset 3/4"

19 g. galvanized 1/2" wire mesh 36" x 36"

Box Assembly

1. Place one wire mesh floor section on the site where the box will sit.
2. Set one end panel (see diagram) on the wire mesh where the back of the box is to be located.
3. Set one side panel adjacent to the end panel, fitting the corners together as shown in the diagram. Screw the two panels together with two screws. Repeat for second side panel.
4. Place the front panel on the fourth side and fit the corners as shown in the diagram. Using 6 screws, attach the front panel to the box.
5. Before filling, square the box to ensure that the lid fits.

Worm Bins

Apartment and townhouse dwellers can become composters on a very small scale by setting up a worm bin on the balcony or in the

Rodent-proof compost box. (This lid is not as strong as the one with cross pieces below.)

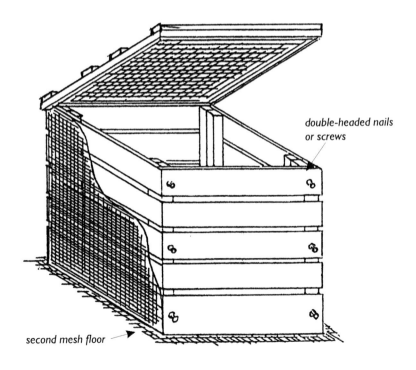

double-headed nails
or screws

second mesh floor

carport. The resulting compost or worm manure can be used for enriching potting soil, topping up planter boxes or fertilizing flower and shrub beds or lawns.

Start with a 6 cu. ft. to 8 cu. ft. plastic bin or equivalent cedar box complete with lid. Drill four to six 3/8″ diameter holes in the bottom of the bin to allow for drainage. Place two pieces of 2x4 wooden planks under the bin so there is room to slide a pot saucer under the drain holes. Add 3″ to 4″ of wet leaves, mulch or damp shredded newspaper to the bin to act as worm bedding and then add your first 4-litre ice cream bucket of kitchen waste. You will have to purchase your pound of red wiggler worms from a supplier or go to a friend with a good functioning compost box and beg enough worms to fill a 1 lb. margarine container. Add the worms to the bin and they will immediately go to work and eat the kitchen waste.

My first worm bin was a 4 cu. ft. cedar box to which I added two to four gallons of kitchen waste each week for four months. The worms reduced the volume to about 1 cu. ft. of finished compost.

Worm bin for composting kitchen waste.

The easiest way to separate the worms from the finished compost when it is time to use it is to pull all the old material to one side of the box and add new compost to the other side. The worms will migrate to the new kitchen waste and abandon the old compost, which can then be removed and used. Any liquid in the drip pan can be diluted by half (add an equivalent amount of water) and used as a liquid fertilizer.

One-year-old compost from a compost box, ready for spring garden.

CHAPTER THREE

Fertilizers

Plant Food Comes in Many Forms

The Fertilizer Act of Canada defines fertilizer as "any substance or mixture of substances containing nitrogen, phosphorous, potassium or other plant food, manufactured, sold or represented for use as a plant nutrient."

Manufacturers or sellers of fertilizer are required by law to clearly label the plant nutrients as a percentage of the total in the fertilizer being sold. All fertilizer containers have three numbers representing the major plant nutrients as a percentage of the total, and possible micro nutrients, if they exist, listed below as parts per thousand (ppt) or parts per million (ppm). Hence a bag of 4.10.10 fertilizer will have 4% nitrogen, 10% phosphorous (phosphorous pentoxide P_2O_5) and 10% potassium (potassium oxide K_2O). This is called the N.P.K ratio and the N.P.K letters come from the Latin symbols for these elements. However, if you measure the pure elemental form of fertilizer in a 16.16.16 fertilizer you find that a 100 lb. bag would contain 16 lb. of nitrogen, 6.88 lbs. of pure phosphorous and 13.28 lb. of pure potassium.

Plants actually require sixteen elements for healthy growth. A shortage of one or more of these sixteen elements may retard or prevent healthy growth. Three elements are supplied by nature and are not generally considered to be fertilizers. Oxygen is taken from air, hydrogen is extracted from water and carbon from carbon dioxide in the air. Additional carbon dioxide can be administered to plants to enhance growth in closed environments such as greenhouses.

The three primary elements, nitrogen, phosphorous and potassium, are found in soil or supplied by some form of fertilizer. Three secondary elements, calcium, magnesium and sulphur, required by plants in lesser amounts, are also found in soil or supplied by fertilizer. The remaining six elements are referred to as micro-nutrients and are required in very small amounts. They may be found naturally in the soil, or added by applying fertilizer with trace elements or adding a specific amendment containing the trace elements. They are boron, chlorine, copper, iron, manganese, molybdenum and zinc.

Until the end of the nineteenth century almost all fertilizers were derived from natural sources such as manures, compost, fish, ground bones or crop rotation. In spite of the atmosphere being 80% nitrogen, plants cannot extract nitrogen from the air. It was not until German chemists developed a method of producing nitrogen compounds for the manufacture of explosives that the artificial fertilizer industry came into prominence.

At the end of the twentieth century many gardeners and agriculturists are going back to the idea of using only natural or organic sources of fertilizer. Plants probably do not know the difference between a chemical or organic source of nitrogen, however, the effect that the type of fertilizer has on the health of the plant and the entire soil ecosystem is significant. No doubt the controversy over fertilizer sources and their value will continue for some time. Information on both types of fertilizer is included later in this chapter.

Roles Played by Fertilizer Elements

Nitrogen (N)
Most important for growth, colour and production of chlorophyll. High demand usually comes between seedling stage and maturity, or when the plant sets seed. Nitrogen is the element

most prone to leach out of the soil with excess irrigation or heavy rainfall. Plants absorb nitrogen primarily in the form of nitrate ions (NO_3) because they are more mobile in the soil. Ammonium ions (NH_4) are also absorbed but are less mobile in soil. Soil bacteria will convert ammonium ions into nitrate ions when temperature, aeration and moisture conditions are favourable. This is one reason why it is so important to maintain a healthy soil environment for microbial activity.

Phosphorous (P)

Helps to form roots, stems, flowers, seeds and fruit. High demand for phosphorus comes in the first stage of a plant's growth from germination to a large seedling. Phosphorous regulates the intake of nitrogen and provides vigour and resistance to disease. Phosphorous is the least likely to leach from the soil. Plants can absorb phosphate ions in three different forms (H_2PO_4, HPO_4, PO_4) determined by the soil's pH. The higher the soil pH (alkaline) the more likely the phosphate will be bound up with other elements and not available to plants. This is a good reason to keep your soil pH at an acceptable level, around 6.5.

Potassium (K)

Helps to strengthen the plant when roots and fruit are being formed, and it increases root growth. Potassium also increases disease resistance and hardens plants against winter cold. There is high demand for potassium in the third stage of growth when fruit is forming and ripening. Potassium will leach less than nitrogen but far more than phosphorous. Plants absorb potassium as potassium ions, which do not bond with other ions to form other compounds.

Calcium (Ca)

Calcium is a structural component of cell walls and membranes and is essential for new cell development and the strength of new plant tissue.

Magnesium (Mg)

Magnesium is one element in the chlorophyll molecule and is therefore necessary for photosynthesis to take place. It also plays a role in the production of various plant enzymes.

Sulphur (S)

Sulphur is absorbed by plants as SO_4 through roots or leaves. It is necessary for the synthesis of proteins and becomes part of a number of amino acids in plants.

Boron (B)

Boron helps cell differentiation in the meristem areas of plants such as shoot tips, root tips and leaf edges. It also plays a role in regulating carbohydrate metabolism in plant cells.

Chlorine (Cl)

Chlorine plays a role in photosynthesis within plant cells.

Copper (Cu)

Copper activates various plant enzyme systems and is necessary for the production of proteins.

Iron (Fe)

Iron is essential for the production of chlorophyll, respiration and nitrogen fixation.

Manganese (Mn)

Manganese is necessary for the production of enzymes that regulate different growth processes and the formation of chlorophyll.

Molybdenum (Mo)

Important in nitrogen utilization that leads to the production of amino acids and proteins. It is also required by nitrogen fixing bacteria on leguminous roots.

Zinc (Zn)

Zinc plays a role in the production of enzymes and plant hormones.

Symptoms of Deficiencies

When fertilizer elements are deficient in soils, plants tend to show characteristic symptoms. Listed below are some of the symptoms that show up as a result of a fertilizer deficiency:

Nitrogen
- Sickly yellow-green leaves with darker green veins, a condition called chlorosis.
- Underside of stem becomes bluish-purple, plant is weak and spindly.
- Slow, stunted growth, lower leaves fall off and fruit is small or poorly formed.

Phosphorous
- Purple or reddish colour on underside of leaf, midrib or stem especially on older leaves.
- Lack of flowers, stunted roots and plant growth.

Potassium
- Symptoms usually appear at the end of the season.
- Mottling, spotting and streaking starts on lower leaves.
- Lower leaves turn grey-green, then bronze or yellowish-brown.
- Brown leaf margins cup downwards and new leaves are crinkled or curled.
- Fruit will be small, thin-skinned and uneven in ripening pattern. (e.g. green shoulders on tomatoes).
- Reduced immunity to disease.

Calcium
- Young leaves yellow and then brown with the tips curling upwards.
- Roots are short, stems weak and growth retarded.
- Responsible for celery and potato blackheart, softness in potatoes during storage, and blossom end rot in melons, peppers, squash and tomatoes.

Magnesium
- Symptoms usually appear at the end of the season.
- Lower leaves become chlorotic, brittle and curl upwards.
- Fruit maturity delayed.

Sulphur
- Lower leaves turn yellow.
- Stems and leaves are hard, brittle and thinner than normal.

Boron
- Symptoms most noticeable in spring when young foliage turns purple or black.
- Growing tips curl inwards, darken and die.
- Plant becomes bushy where new growth has started below dead growing tips.
- Midribs and leaf stems are brittle.
- Fruit fails to mature and drops or forms corky spots.
- Responsible for heartrot and blackheart in celery, beets and turnips and hollow stems in broccoli, cauliflower and cabbage.

Copper
- Terminal growth yellows, withers and falls in mid-June (wither tip).
- Lettuce leaves can become overly long (rabbit's ear).
- Pockets of sap may exude from plant.
- Lack of vigour and dwarfing in conifers.

Iron

- Chlorotic leaves begin to form at the top of the plant.
- Leaves turn pale green and plant lacks vigour.
- Similar to anemia in humans.

Manganese

- Chlorosis on young leaves but not the same as for iron deficiency.
- Leaves will wither and die and plant growth is retarded.
- Soils rich in organics (muck soils) with a pH of 6 to 7.5 tend to be deficient in manganese.

Molybdenum

- Broccoli and cauliflower leaves become long, twisted and narrow (whiptail).
- Leaves yellow and fold inward and plant is stunted.

Zinc

- Foliage is thin and small and some buds do not form.
- Distance between internodes is very short so plant looks stunted and distorted.
- Some foliage may have dead spots.

An excess of a fertilizer element can be as big a problem as a deficiency. A fertilizer element can create a toxicity in plants or burn the roots if the concentration of dissolved fertilizer salts is too high. For example, excessive magnesium prevents the uptake of potassium and this can create a deficiency. More and more gardeners are realizing that plant health and resistance to disease is often regulated by the right balance of fertilizer elements and beneficial microbes.

Organic Fertilizers

Organic fertilizers are generally less concentrated and slower to release, thereby creating less potential to accumulate in the soil and harm the soil microbes. As the demand grows for more organic fertilizers, many companies are now producing commercial organic fertilizers for both agricultural use and home gardeners.

Sources of Organic Fertilizer by Product

Blood Meal
Dried and ground blood from slaughtered animals that is quick acting (14.1.0).

Bone Meal
Animal bones that are treated with high temperature steam, then dried, ground and screened. Bone meal has a very slow release time (2.14.0).

Compost, Humus and Leaf Mould
Created by nature or the product of a composting operation.

Composted Manure
Animal manure that has been composted by heating, turning and aging.

Composted Tankage
Food, fruit and vegetable wastes that have been composted in large enclosed vats or tanks.

Fish Meal
Tissue, bone and other fish waste treated with live steam, dried and ground. Fish emulsion is a similar product in liquid form (5.3.3).

Gelatin
A source of nitrogen but may mould after being dissolved and poured on soil (4.0.0).

Green Manure
Nitrogen-rich or nitrogen-fixing crops grown for the purpose of being plowed under before the main crop is planted.

Hoof and Horn
Ground animal waste and a source of nitrogen-like gelatin.

Manure
Fresh or dried animal or bird excreta.

Peat
Partly decayed vegetable matter that is classified as sphagnum or sedge, has very little nutrient and can be very acidic.

Seaweed and Kelp
A good source of liquid or solid fertilizer that is weed- and pathogen-free and rich in trace elements (1.5-0.5-2.5).

Sewage
Tertiary treated sewage sludge that has been screened, dried and ground.

Meals
- Vegetable Meals, such as Canola and Alfalfa - (5.1.2).
- Crab, Prawn and Shrimp Meal.
- Feather Meal (Ground poultry feathers (11.0.0).)
- Worm Castings or Worm Manure - (0.5, 0.5, 0.3).

Other natural sources of inorganic fertilizers: ground soft and hard rock phosphate (0.18.0); granite dust (rich in trace elements) (0.0.4); greensand (iron silicate, potassium and rich in trace elements) (0.0.7); wood ash (potassium carbonate); potassium sulphate (0.0.52).

Manures

Until the early part of the 20th century, manures were the primary source of fertilizer. With the introduction of chemical fertilizers and the mechanization of agriculture, both the amount of manure and the need for manure diminished rapidly. Today, with the expansion of feedlots, manure has once again become plentiful and in some cases has become a major environmental problem.

The quality of manure will vary greatly depending on the species of animal, the fodder they are eating and the method of storage. Manure piles that have gone anaerobic or have been left out in the winter rains will not be a good product. In addition to adding basic nutrients to the soil, manures act as a good soil conditioner and source of microbial life.

Manure Sources

Cool Manures
Manures that come from most large farm animals have a lower percentage of nitrogen and are less likely to burn plant roots when added in a fresh state.

Cow
Most commercial manure, bagged or bulk, comes from feedlot operations and is marketed as steer manure. Technically speaking, it is not pure steer manure because steers are castrated male cows (oxen) and feedlots have both male and female cattle. Feed lots use large amounts of sawdust to soak up the urine and keep the cows dry. Unfortunately, a good portion of the nitrogen in the manure is used by the bacteria that breaks down the sawdust.

Most bagged steer manure has been composted and then blended with peat moss to extend it and to reduce the potential for burning when used by inexperienced gardeners. In most cases the nutrient value is very low.

In earlier days it was not uncommon for home gardeners to bring in a load of fresh manure from the country and spread it on the garden. To do this today in most suburban areas would not make you popular with your neighbours because of the strong smell. Ideally cow manure should be aged for eight months to a year, or composted before being used as a soil amendment. Of all the manures it is one of the best and most widely used. Dairy manure will generally have fewer nutrients than steer manure because of the cow's diet. The N P K would be N (1- 2.5 %), P (.9 - 1.6 %) and K (2.4 - 3.6 %).

Horse

Before the advent of the motorcar, there was no shortage of horse manure. Today the supply of horse manure in urban areas comes mainly from riding stables. Like feedlots there is a great deal of sawdust mixed with the manure and this reduces its value. Horses, unlike cows, have only one stomach and much of the fodder (40%+) is not fully digested as it passes through the horse. If their fodder is full of grass or weed seeds, then adding horse manure to your garden can be disastrous. Horse manure is rich in ammonia (N), which will cause it to heat rapidly if composted in sufficient quantities. The heat from the hot composting should kill most of the weed seeds. This ability of horse manure to generate heat was widely used for creating "hot beds" below cold frames in Victorian gardens.

Sheep

Some sheep manure may be available from hobby farms and is very rich if not mixed with too much bedding. When fresh and wet, the smell can be a problem.

Pig

Although rich, manure from hogs is extremely smelly and is not suitable for use on suburban gardens unless well composted and aged.

Hot Manures

Manures that are rich in nitrogen and are prone to burn roots when added as fresh manure or in too great a quantity.

Chicken

This manure is very smelly when wet but can be stored in a dry form. It is very rich in nitrogen and will burn plants if applied directly to the root area. It is best composted or used as a manure tea and applied sparingly to those plants where green top growth is desired. Other bird manures such as turkey, duck, geese and pigeon are all similar to chicken. Nitrogen (2 - 4.5%), Phosphorous (4.6 - 6%), Potassium (1.2 - 2.4%).

Rabbit

Not generally available unless you own rabbits, but it is rich in nitrogen.

Mushroom Manure

This is a misnomer and is more accurately called mushroom compost. The compost is prepared from horse manure, chicken manure, straw, peanut shells and a variety of other materials that may be available. After a high temperature composting process, the mushroom compost is loaded into trays in a temperature and humidity-controlled barn where the mushroom spawn (spores) is added. When the new crop of mushrooms has extracted most of the nutrients from the compost, the residue becomes a waste product and is sold to soil companies, landscapers and gardeners as an organic amendment. The pH of mushroom compost can be very high when fresh and should not be used on ericaceous plants such as rhododendrons.

Chemical Fertilizers

There are many forms of artificial or chemical fertilizers on the market. They are highly concentrated, generally granulated and easy to apply but may not be the best for the long term biological health of the soil. If the N.P.K. ratio of a chemical fertilizer is 12.18.15 it may only take a small handful of granules to fertilize a plant. Compost, on the other hand, may have an N.P.K. of 1-0.5-0.5 and have a very slow release rate, which means you will need a pail full or a wheelbarrow full of compost to get the same nutrient value. Concentrated liquid fertilizers are expensive and need to be diluted with water but are quick acting because they are absorbed by the foliage or permeate the root zone immediately. Unfortunately, they will also leach out of soil more quickly and are therefore more often used for houseplants or container plants.

There are two general types of slow-release fertilizers. One is encapsulated in a polymer or resin that will only begin to release fertilizer when the capsule becomes wet and absorbs water. The water dissolves the fertilizer and expands the polymer. However, temperature regulates the rate of expansion and the fertilizer is not released until the temperature reaches 20°C. The rate of release increases as the temperature increases. By changing the thickness or composition of the polymer, the rate of release can vary from 3 to 10 months. The other type of slow-release fertilizer is coated with a material such as sulphur, allowing for a very slow rate of release due to moisture and microbial activity on the sulphur.

Chemical Sources of Fertilizer Elements

Sources of Nitrogen
- Ammonium Nitrate (33%).
- Ammonium Sulphate (26%): slow to release, requires bacterial action.
- Calcium Nitrate (21%).

- Sodium Nitrate (16%): also known as Chile Saltpeter.
- Urea Formaldehyde (46%): not soluble in water, bacteria breaks down urea into ammonium compounds.

Sources of Phosphorous
- Slag from blast furnaces (8-16%): slow acting.
- Super phosphate (20%): soluble and acts quickly.
- Triple super phosphate (46%): soluble and acts quickly.

Sources of Potassium
- Potassium Chloride (60%): soluble and acts quickly.
- Potassium Nitrate (45%).
- Potassium Sulphate (50%): also known as Sulphate of Potash, soluble and acts quickly.

Sources of Calcium
- Limestone - composed of calcium carbonate, grey in colour (95% calcium carbonate).
- Dolomite Limestone: composed of calcium and magnesium carbonate, white in colour (51% calcium carbonate and 40% magnesium carbonate).
- Agricultural Lime: limestone that has been burned in a kiln to produce calcium oxide is then added to water to form calcium hydroxide. The calcium hydroxide is ground into powder and sold as lime. It is very alkaline, quick-acting and prone to burn roots.
- Gypsum: calcium sulphate is sometimes used to help break up heavy clay soils.

Sources of Other Fertilizer Elements
- Aluminum Sulphate (18%): used to acidify soil.
- Borax: used to treat soils that are deficient in boron.
- Frittered Trace Elements (FTE): six trace elements in soft glass pellets that break down very slowly and release micronutrients.

- Iron Chelates (13%): soluble iron that is tightly bonded to an organic compound that will provide a source of slow release iron.
- Iron Sulphate (30%): used to treat chlorosis and as a moss killer.
- Magnesium Sulphate (10%): also known as Epsom Salts and used to treat magnesium deficiencies.
- Elemental Sulphur: used to treat soils deficient in sulphur and to acidify soil.

The Relationship Between Soil Particles, Fertilizers and Plants

There is a close relationship between the soil's physical and chemical properties and the growth of plants. Clay and humus are the most chemically active particles in soil. The very small clay and humus particles in soil are called colloids and have weak electrical charges on their surfaces. They can be either positive or negative but colloids in mid-latitude garden soils are mostly negative. The nutrients that plants require are in ionic form and are attracted to opposite charges. Since colloids have a negative charge they attract and hold.

This is called the cation exchange capacity or CEC. This helps to explain why clay soils and soils with higher organic content are more fertile. Colloids in low pH soils have lower negative charges and less ability to hold positive fertilizer cations. Cation exchange occurs when positive cations such as calcium, magnesium or potassium are displaced from colloids by hydrogen

Ions and Charges

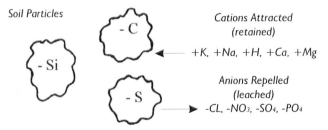

Soil Particles

- C

- Si

- S

Cations Attracted
(retained)

+K, +Na, +H, +Ca, +Mg

Anions Repelled
(leached)

-CL, -NO₃, -SO₄, -PO₄

cations that have been deposited in the soil by plants. The Ca, Mg and K cations are then free and can be absorbed as nutrients by plants.

In an ideal world we would all be able to garden in a light friable loam that is well drained, has the right amount of organic material and is rich in nutrients. Unfortunately, this is seldom the case. Most soils require amendments to create the right texture, organic content and level of nutrients. Most nutrients are held in the soil by electrical charges or bonding. Some soils are better at holding these particles than others. Clay soils are better than sandy soils and those soils with high organic content are even better.

In dry areas with minimum rainfall, soil moisture is pulled to the surface by capillary action and evaporated. This leaves soluble salts on the surface, making the soil quite alkaline and in some cases unusable. Land that has been irrigated for half a century often has to be taken out of production for a year or two and flooded to leach out the concentration of accumulated salts.

Conversely, high rainfall areas are prone to leaching and the soluble fertilizer salts end up in the subsoil or in local streams and lakes. Natural carbon dioxide in the air combines with rainwater and forms a very weak solution of carbonic acid which acidifies the soil along with acid rain from pollution.

Having your soil tested for pH and available nutrients is probably more important in areas where there is less rainfall. In high rainfall areas most new or unamended soils will have a low pH and will be deficient in fertilizer salts, particularly nitrogen.

Testing soils for pH or basic nutrients with an inexpensive probe or soil test kit is next to useless. Most major urban centres have soil testing labs that will do basic tests for a nominal fee. Ideally it would be useful to test for soil biology (microbes) as well as for chemistry (nutrients) but, unfortunately, there are not enough qualified labs to do the biology work.

How to Take a Soil Sample

The data you receive will only be as good as the soil sample you submit. Each soil sample should represent only one soil type, soil condition or management history. The sample should be representative of the soil from 3 to 22 cm or the depth of cultivation. Take sub-samples from 10 to 15 locations and then thoroughly mix all the soil into a half litre representative sample. Avoid soils that have been recently fertilized, have encrusted salt accumulations or are in low areas that collect runoff water. Use clean sampling tools that are not galvanized, copper or bronze, and clean glass or plastic containers.

How to Read a Soil Analysis Report

Most soil analysis reports will have the following items listed:

pH

Indicates the acidity or alkalinity of a soil sample. Most garden soils should be about 6.5 (slightly acidic) on a scale of 1 to 14 where 7 is neutral.

% Breakdown of Soil Particles

Sand, silt and clay as a percentage or silt and clay will be listed together as *fines*. This will give an indication as to the type of loam you are working with and its characteristics.

E.C. or Electrical Conductivity

The higher the electrical conductivity in soil, the higher the level of fertilizer salts. Salt in solution forms an electrolyte and the stronger the solution the better the conductivity. A reading of 0 to 2 would be low, 2 to 3 would be normal, 3 to 4 approaching the danger level and above 4 would be harmful to most plants.

Organic Matter
This is expressed as a percentage of the total sample weight. 10% to 20% is considered to be appropriate for most soils. Too much organic matter can result in excessive water retention, shallow roots and compaction from foot traffic. Too little will result in poor soil structure, low microbial activity, inability to hold water, and poor natural fertility.

Carbon to Nitrogen Ratio
This becomes important when you are dealing with natural soils that have a high organic content, or manufactured soils that are compost-based and may have a significant amount of partially decayed wood. Ratios of more than 40:1 may indicate that you need to add additional nitrogen for good growth.

Fertilizer Elements Available
These will be listed as a percentage, ppt or ppm. Some reports will list nitrogen, nitrate nitrogen and ammonium nitrogen separately. Many soil analysis sheets use 1 as a base figure and then rate each element in relation to 1 as being the ideal level. (If the number is .5 there is half of what is ideal, if it is 2 then the concentration is twice what it should be.) The normal range or rough averages in garden soils for these fertilizer elements are listed below:
- **Nitrogen:** Measured as nitrogen - 0 to 20 ppm is low, 20 to 50 ppm is medium and 50 or more is high in dry soil.
- **Phosphorous:** Measured as P_2O_5 - 0 to 12 ppm is low, 12 to 25 is medium and 25 or more is high.
- **Potassium:** Measured as K_2O - 0 to 50 is low, 50 to 100 is medium, and more than 100 is high.
- **Calcium:** Measured as Ca - 0 to 30 is low, 30 to 60 is medium, and above 60 is high.
- **Magnesium** (measured as magnesium): 0 to 20 is low, 20 to 30 is medium, and 30 or more is high.
- **Copper:** 8 to 30 ppm

Soil Analysis Sheet

Client

	pH potential hydrogen ions	EC electrical conductivity	OM organic matter	N nitrogen	P phosphorus	K potassium	Ca calcium	Mg magnesium	Cu copper	Zn zinc	Fe iron	Mn manganese	B boron	S sulfur	NH_4 ammonium	NO_3 nitrate	Na sodium
Example																	
Top Soil																	
Sample																	
% sand 65%																	
% fines 20%																	
C/N Ratio 24																	
Comments	See page 51 for range of readings for each element																

- **Zinc:** 25 to 75 ppm
- **Iron:** 100 to 300 ppm
- **Manganese:** 50 to 100 ppm
- **Boron:** 8 to 20 ppm
- **Sulphur:** 25 to 50
- **Molybdenum**: not generally measured

What's Going On Down There?

Most plants live in two worlds, one visible above ground and one invisible below ground. The root or section of the plant below ground serves two purposes: to anchor the plant, and to feed the plant. The only way roots can absorb food is in liquid form or a solution of fertilizer salts and water. The only parts of the root that can do this efficiently are the tiny root hairs found at the growing tips.

When fertilizer salts from chemical or organic sources are dissolved, they form tiny particles called ions that attach themselves to soil particles or bits of organic material. Minute clay particles and compost have a greater capacity to attract and hold these ions and hence prevent the fertilizer ions from being leached from the soil. Larger sand particles do not have the ability to hold ions. This is one reason why it is important to add compost or organic matter to soil.

A plant growing in soil that has sufficient rainfall or is well irrigated will have no trouble absorbing dissolved fertilizer salts. This occurs through a process called osmosis in which the salt solution inside the root cell is more concentrated than the salt solution in the soil. The less dense solution in the soil is absorbed through the cell membrane into the more dense solution in the cell. The absorbed ions or nutrients are then transported to various parts of the plant by vessels or xylem cells.

Problems with this feeding system can occur when the soil

dries out or when the concentration of fertilizer salts becomes too high. When the soil dries out there is no moisture to transport the nutrients into the roots and the plant is starved for nutrients. A good example of this is when tomato plants dry out: the uptake of calcium seizes and the tomato develops blossom end rot. In response to this problem, garden books often suggest you add lime or that you don't let your plants dry out, but fail to explain the inter-connection between the two.

If the fertilizer solution in the soil becomes too strong, either through lack of moisture which concentrates the fertilizer, or because of additions of excess fertilizer, reverse osmosis takes place and the moisture in the root cells is pulled out, causing the root cell to be short of moisture or to collapse. A shortage of moisture will cause the plant to wilt temporarily but if the cell totally collapses, the root turns black and appears to have been burned. In some cases where high concentrations of fertilizer are absorbed into the roots and transported to the leaves, the "burning" shows up on the edges of the leaves due to transpiration or water loss.

When applying fertilizer, be sure to spread it evenly around the drip line of the plant where the root hairs are located, not near the stem or trunk. Cultivate the soil before you water in the fertilizer to prevent high concentrations of salts from forming too close to the roots.

The pH of soil does not generally affect the roots directly but does have a major influence on the availability of various fertilizer elements that the roots can absorb. For example, as the soil becomes more acidic, iron and manganese are freed up, but magnesium is tied up, which may cause a deficiency. Adding lime will correct the pH problem and a dilute solution of Epsom Salts will help correct the deficiency. The reverse is true for alkaline soils. An iron deficiency is referred to as chlorosis and can be corrected by using chelated iron, which binds the iron to soluble ions. It is then available to plants through their roots.

Understanding the relationship between roots, nutrients and pH will help with soil improvement, watering, fertilizing, diagnosing nutrient deficiencies and will, ultimately, lead to healthier plants.

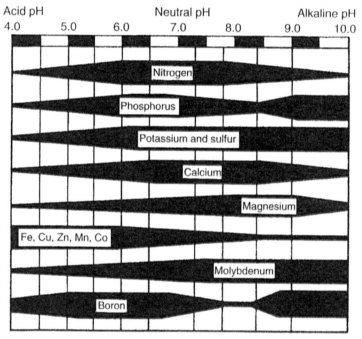

Soil reaction chart (pH) indicates availability of nutrients at various pH readings.

CHAPTER FOUR

Mulches
Garden Blankets

I n the natural world, almost all vegetative areas will have some form of organic covering on the soil surface. Conifer needles, broad leaves, rotting logs and dead grass may accumulate over the years to form material referred to under a variety of names, such as forest floor debris, leaf mould, duff, thatch or humus. This is nature's way of protecting the soil from the elements, providing a habitat for micro-organisms to break down dead vegetation, slowly feeding the plants with organic fertilizer and helping to conserve moisture. Mulches added to the home garden provide the same benefits as natural organic coverings but are added to the garden very quickly.

A 2 to 4 cm thick mulch applied in the fall will act as a blanket or insulator to prevent frost from penetrating the soil and damaging tender roots. Piling a thick layer of dead leaves over the plant can also protect stems and sprouts above ground.

For example, trailing tender fuchsia in a window box can be cut down to 10 to 15 cm and then packed in lawn moss (a product of power raking the lawn) before being covered with a plastic sheet and a 10 to 15 cm layer of dead fern fronds. A snowfall on top of the fronds during very cold weather will also act as a good insulator. Sub-tropical plants, such as the roots of a hardy banana, can be left in the ground over the winter in zone 8 areas if they are covered with 60 to 90 cm of leaves, retained in a chicken wire circle and capped with a plastic covering to keep them dry. *(See Zone Chart on page 80.)*

Adding a similar 10 to 15 cm layer of mulch to garden beds in the summertime has the opposite effect. In this case it becomes an insulator against heat and keeps root structures cool. For example, clematis and lilies prefer a cool area for their root structures and benefit from a good layer of mulch if planted on the south side of a house. A thick layer of mulch can retard normal growth in spring or summer for heat-loving plants.

A coarse mulch on a newly planted area will help prevent soil heaving from frost and compaction due to the pounding effect of heavy rainfall. If the garden area is on a slope, a coarse mulch will help to prevent soil movement and erosion.

A rich organic mulch will foster the growth of microbial life in the mulch and the soil below. As the microbes and worms break down the mulch and turn it into valuable top soil, they also release a wide range of beneficial nutrients for plants. Dead or decaying organic material that falls to the ground and forms a mulch has exactly the right combination of nutrients that the plant above requires. This recycling of nutrients completes the biological cycle that is often lacking in home gardens. Instead of leaving the dead rhododendron leaves under the plant as a mulch, too many gardeners rake the area clean and send the leaves to the landfill. It makes more sense to leave the dead leaves under the plant as a mulch or rake them up, grind them with a rotary lawn mower and then place them back under the rhododendron plant.

Conservation of moisture is becoming more and more of an issue with global warming and dwindling supplies. Using less water and conserving what is available makes good sense. The coarse nature of mulches helps to prevent evaporation by reducing capillary action. Observing an apparatus called capillary tubes will help demonstrate the principle. When five glass tubes all the same length but with different internal diameters ranging from 1 mm to 5 mm are placed in an upright position and attached to the same reservoir filled with coloured water, each tube will pull water up the tube by capillary action. The distance the water is pulled up the tube is determined by the interior diameter of the tube, the smaller the tube the higher the water will be pulled. Transferring this scientific phenomenon to soil means that the greater the space between the soil or mulch particles the less able it is to pull water to the surface by capillary action and have it evaporate and lost. Therefore, a coarse mulch helps stop the movement of water from coming to the surface. This simple principle can be observed on newly-tilled soil where the surface soil has had time to dry. If someone walks across the freshly-tilled soil and leaves heavily compacted footprints, the moisture will come to the surface. The soil particles below the footprint are tightly compacted and have greater ability to pull water to the surface by capillary action. Contrary to common belief, cultivating and fluffing soil after a rain actually helps to conserve moisture.

Capillary Tubes
(hollow glass tubes with common reservoir)

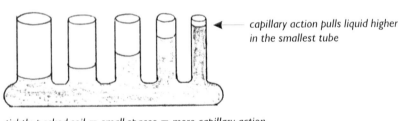

capillary action pulls liquid higher in the smallest tube

tightly-packed soil = small spaces = more capillary action
loosely-packed soil = larger spaces = less capillary action

Soil Evaporation

warm air movement

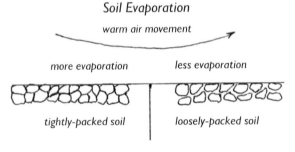

more evaporation   *less evaporation*

tightly-packed soil   *loosely-packed soil*

It is unnatural to have soil surfaces bare during the winter. Mulches keep winter soils warm and prevent compaction. Winter cover crops may do the same thing, as well as holding nutrients in their roots. Spring soils will warm more quickly without a mulch. Summer soils may be covered with mulch if the roots prefer a cool environment.

Mulches can be divided into organic and inorganic. Some are more beneficial for improving topsoil than others, even though they are organic.

Organic Mulches

Home Compost
One of the best because it is free and does not require any transportation. The gardener also knows exactly what it is made from.

Commercial Compost
A product made from residential green waste, food waste and wood waste. Generally of good quality but tends to be coarser than home compost.

Composted Bark Mulch
Dark in colour and will be less inclined than raw bark mulch to rob nitrogen from plants as it continues to decay. May need supplementary nitrogen for good growth.

Raw Bark Mulch (Wood Waste)
Use only fir, hemlock or pine, and avoid cedar. Robs available nitrogen from plants and surface turns grey with age. Prone to be greasy in very wet weather and a fire hazard in hot dry weather. Do not use close to wooden buildings.

Steer Manure
Comes most often from feedlots and may contain an abnormally

high content of sawdust or wood waste. Can be too rich for some plants such as rhododendrons and some of the flowering shrubs.

Horse Manure
Very high content of sawdust or wood waste and is likely to have an abundance of undigested weed seeds.

Straw (stalks from grain crops)
Is slow to break down and can be unsightly except in the vegetable garden.

Hay (stalks from grass plants)
Not recommended because of grass and weed seeds.

Conifer Cones
Are used for semi permanent mulches or ground covers below trees where very little will grow. They are slow to break down and will not add anything to the soil for a very long time.

Newspaper
Used by some vegetable gardeners to retain moisture and reduce weeding. May cause soil to become anaerobic and sour. Will eventually break down but looks unsightly unless you are a compulsive reader.

Spaghnum Peat Moss
Is a good soil conditioner but is expensive. In winter it is prone to hold too much water and in summer, if it dries out, it is almost impossible to re-moisten quickly, short of using a wetting agent.

Inorganic Mulches

Volcanic Rock (red or black)
Used more for decorative purposes or under stairways where nothing will grow.

Stone, Quartz Stone (white), Limestone (grey), River Rock (grey)

Are all used for decorative purposes or where there is heavy foot traffic. Horticultural cloth should be laid down under all rock materials.

Horticultural Cloth

Usually laid down to prevent erosion or as a weed inhibitor. Only the tight weave type will stop the weeds. Best used in conjunction with another organic mulch as a cover. Soil below may become anaerobic.

Black Plastic

Should never be used as a weed inhibitor because it does not allow rain water or oxygen to pass through and surrounding plants will suffer from drought and anaerobic conditions. Poking holes in the plastic will allow water through but it will also allow weeds to grow. Some gardeners use 1m strips to cover the soil in tomato or pepper beds where irrigation is available. The black surface helps to increase the soil temperature for these heat lovers.

CHAPTER FIVE

Plant Structures & Processes

Pollen: All About the Wind and the Bees

For some people spring and summer can be a time of discomfort because of pollen allergies. In spite of the problems pollen causes, pollination is a vital process for our survival in the natural environment, for commercial farming and for home gardening.

As a child I can remember going into the flower garden and hearing the hum of thousands of bees busily working the nectar-rich flowers and carrying sticky pollen from plant to plant. Unfortunately, today one has to look hard to find a single bee in a flowerbed. Without the movement of pollen there will be limited fruit and seeds. Reproduction for some plant species will not happen without the aid of bees.

Fortunately, many plants rely on wind to transfer their pollen. This is true for grasses, grains and corn. However, most of our valuable food crops need insects or bees to pollinate the flowers. Unfortunately, wind-driven pollen is the type that causes the most hay fever.

There are two types of pollination: self-pollination and cross-pollination. Cross-pollination is when pollen, the equivalent of male sperm, from one plant lands on the stigma or receptor of another plant and fertilizes the ovule or undeveloped seed. This process ensures a greater genetic diversity. Natural hybridization between different species will not occur because the outer layer on pollen has a complex pattern on its surface and cannot fuse with the stigma on a foreign plant. In other cases, pollen will release proteins and hormones that do not fit the code the stigma requires to accept fertilization.

To ensure cross-fertilization, many plants are programmed to produce their male and female flowers at different times. If self-pollination does occur, the fruit or seed crop usually will not be as abundant. When trees, such as apples, require cross pollination there must be a neighbouring tree blooming at exactly the right time. This is why it is very important to choose compatible trees.

Holly is a good example of a tree that produces male and female flowers on different plants to ensure there is cross-pollination. This is called *dioecious* after the Greek "two households". Male holly trees will never produce berries as they are only equipped to produce pollen. For some reason, the vast majority of holly seedlings are male and less desirable to grow because they will not produce berries.

Zucchinis are *monoecious* "one household" and have separate male and female flowers on the same plant. Self-pollination will take place providing both types of flowers are open at the same time.

When pollen lands on the moist or sticky surface of the stigma, it germinates and begins to grow a pollen tube into the stigma to reach the ovules. In the case of crocus, the tube can be up to 20 cm long or from the flower down to the *corm*. Once the ovules are fertilized, the seedpod has to grow back up above the ground surface to ripen. In the case of impatiens, the pollen tube can grow within minutes of fertilization. Hormones are often released to soften the host cells and speed the pollen tube growth process. Fertilization draws on nutrients in the sap to form the new seeds and the fruit in which they are encased.

Plants that produce wind-dispersed pollen have not evolved in the same way as insect-dependent plants. The flowers are often very small and inconspicuous, not having to attract insects. Without insects to carry the pollen directly to other plants of the same species, pollen is produced in copious quantities. The receptors for wind-blown pollen are generally well positioned to catch the dust-like particles. The pollen may also have a very rough surface to facilitate sticking to the stigma. This rough surface may be the cause of many peoples' allergies. It is remarkable to think that every kernel of corn has been pollinated by wind-blown pollen and has grown down one of the thousands of tassel fibers.

Conifer trees, grasses and some of the common weeds are well known for wind blown pollen. If you see yellow dust falling on your deck in the late spring it is probably pollen from fir or pine trees.

Pollen can be an aggravation for those who suffer from allergies but to live in a world without it would mean going back to our primeval beginnings.

Roots and Shoots

Have you ever found a bulb or begonia tuber that was planted upside down, and wondered how the roots and stems knew how to change direction and continue growing? Most gardeners have noticed that when a potted plant is knocked over, the growing tip bends and starts to grow upwards. The roots are not visible but they too change direction and start growing downwards.

Up and down growth patterns in plants are all determined by chemical regulators. These regulators are closely related to chemicals in the human body that we call hormones. Unlike the human body, plants do not have special organs that produce special hormones. The hormone-like chemicals are produced in cells found in roots, stems and leaves. Chemicals, or hormones, of a similar nature regulate different aspects of plant growth, depending on where they are found in the plant. The best-known plant hormone or chemical regulator is called *auxin*, a term that comes from the Greek word "to increase".

Auxins will automatically redirect the growing tip up by concentrating at the base of the stem and causing the cells to elongate, thereby forcing the stem to curl and grow upwards.

Conversely, in the roots, auxins collect at the base of the root and retard the cell growth, causing the roots to curl and grow down. Roots also seem to be affected by starch granules that act like marbles in liquid. They sink to the bottom of the cell and influence the auxins and the direction of growth.

When plants grow against gravity it is called *negative geotropism* and when they grow with gravity it is called *positive geotropism*. The geotropic responses built into plants and regulated by auxins are particularly helpful when it comes to planting seeds. Imagine the problem trying to plant every seed right side up so the roots know which way to grow. Fortunately, a seed with the aid of a new root has the ability to pull itself into the right growing position.

There are many common garden practices related to this geotropic phenomenon. Some climbing roses are prone to grow long vertical shoots up in the air where they form few, if any, flowers. Pulling them down and tying them so the tip is closer to the ground will trigger a negative geotropic response and a flush of side shoots that are programmed to flower.

Espaliered fruit trees growing on a horizontal wire will react in a similar way, producing more fruit spurs and a better crop of fruit.

Fruit trees that are not espaliered perform best when their branches are trained down rather than up. Tying a weight on supple branches will bend them down and create a more productive tree.

Vines often produce more flowers after they reach the top of the fence or trellis and grow horizontally or cascade down.

Climbing plants with either tendrils or twining behaviour also rely on chemical regulators. Grapes and peas, for instance, use tendrils to support plants in an area where they will get the most sunlight. When a tendril touches a stake or string, it immediately wants to wrap itself around the support. This behaviour is called *thigmotropism* and results from a stimulus to touch and, possibly, a reaction to darkness. The cells elongate on the non-contact side and the tendril starts to curl around the stake or wire. The auxins may also affect the turgor of the tendril to help the curling action, which can be quite rapid.

Twining plants respond to negative geotropism but have the additional characteristic of wanting to grow slightly more on one side of the stem than the other, and this causes them to twine. In the case of wisteria, the Chinese variety twines clockwise while the Japanese variety wants to go counter-clockwise. I don't think botanists have figured this one out yet.

Getting to know more about the behaviour of plants may help produce better specimens and give you greater satisfaction pursuing your gardening hobby.

Why Leaves Change Colour

After a long dry summer one does not expect a great display of fall colour, unless the rains come in time to allow trees and shrubs to recharge their moisture supply required to put on a beautiful show.

While most people enjoy the annual display of fall colours, they may not have thought about why it happens. There are a number of conditions that determine the colours we see.

During the summer when growing conditions are ideal, leaves are busy converting nutrients into food with the aid of sunlight and a green chemical called *chlorophyll*. The presence of chlorophyll gives the leaf its characteristic green colour. Leaves of a different colour still contain chlorophyll but other pigments in the leaf tissue mask it.

In the fall when light levels change and night time temperatures begin to drop, deciduous trees and shrubs are triggered to quickly move as much food as possible from the leaves to the roots for winter storage. The production of chlorophyll stops and the green pigment drains away. Some of the remaining glucose or sugar will convert to a chemical called *anthocyanins*, a red pigment, which actually assists with the rapid movement of food from the leaf. This is the same pigment that is found in red radishes and beets.

Once most of the food or carbohydrates and albumin have moved out of the leaf, the tubes or veins at the tip of the leaf stem close off, trapping any remaining sugar or glucose and pigments in the leaf. These naturally occurring pigments are yellow granules containing carotenes and xanthophylls. They are the same yellow pigments that are found in bananas, oranges, carrots and pumpkins.

When leaves lack pigment, they generally turn brown, shrivel up and fall off. With a modest amount of yellow pigment, such as is found in Poplar trees, the leaves turn a bright yellow.

When anthocyanins, red pigment, is also present and mixed with the yellow, the leaves turn bright orange. An abundance of red pigment will create fiery red leaves. Not all the anthocyanins show up as red pigment. When the sap in the leaf is neutral or slightly alkaline a blue pigment is formed. When the sap is slightly acid the pigment will be violet. This is why some leaves have a deep reddish-purple colour before they drop. However, when the sap is distinctly acid, the typical red pigment is produced.

Leaf colour also depends on a number of external factors. Sunlight is essential and will help determine the intensity of the colour. Tests have been done on leaves using tape to block out the sunlight. The patch under the tape fails to develop colour and goes brown.

Cooling air will trigger the colouring process but a heavy frost will arrest the whole process and cause the leaves to drop.

Lack of moisture will also cause the leaves to turn brown and fall prematurely. This is what happens in the tropics during the dry season when there is no cold weather to trigger a colour change, and what might happen if rain does not come in September.

A difference in mineral content in the soil may also have a minor impact on leaf colour.

Each species of tree reacts differently to the various triggering mechanisms. Some react quickly and start their colour change in late August or early September while others don't react until November. The majority of landscaping trees in coastal areas seems to be at their best in the second or third week of October. As you go inland or north, the show of colours begins earlier.

There are very few deciduous coniferous trees. Needles of both Western Larch (Larix occidentalis) and Swamp Cypress (Taxodium distichum) turn a bright yellow and then brown before they drop. Other conifers such as Cryptomeria japonica and some of the Thujas (Cedars) develop a distinct purple-brown hue as the cold weather sets in and pigments start to form in the foliage.

CHAPTER SIX

Photoperiodism
& Light Exposure
Let There Be Light

Winter, with its short days and long nights, is not an ideal time for growing plants. However, to have bedding plants such as geraniums ready for transplanting in May, the seed must be planted in January. So it is necessary that a good supplementary source of light be provided.

Light is characterized by wave length or colour on the electro-magnetic spectrum. Short wave or *ultra-violet* light is at one end of the spectrum and long wave or *infrared* is at the other end. Waves beyond both ends of the visible spectrum cannot be seen by the human eye but may be detectable by individual plant cells.

Dr. John Ott, an American researcher who worked with time-lapse photography, devised a number of experiments to show how dependent plants are on full spectrum light and how they have adapted to certain light conditions. The use of narrow spectrum photographic lights in his work made him aware of some of these problems.

When he worked with a pumpkin plant for the Disney movie, "Secrets of Life," he found that female flowers would die if they only had red light whereas the same was true for male flowers when given only blue light. On another project he found morning-glory flower buds would collapse and die before they bloomed if they were exposed to red light during the night.

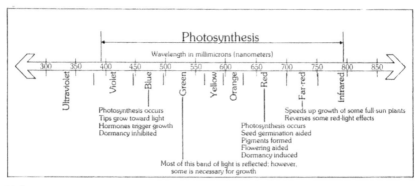

Light spectrum

Hothouse tomatoes grown during the short cloudy days of winter were much more susceptible to virus diseases. When he took young infected plants from the greenhouse and exposed them to a full spectrum light, the plants' health returned to normal. With full spectrum light, normal *photosynthesis* could take place and prevent the abnormal chemistry that encouraged virus development.

Some fruit, such as tomatoes, can be picked and placed in a dark cupboard and they will turn red and ripen. Other fruit like apples need ultra-violet light to trigger the colouring. Sunny days in the late summer or fall are essential if the apple crop is to turn red.

It has long been known that the blooming period of many plants is triggered by the length of the day. Poinsettia is brought into flower for the Christmas season by shortening their daylight period to less than 12 hours. Chrysanthemums are available all year round as potted plants by manipulating the length of day using black blinds in greenhouses.

When Dr. Ott did some film work on *Hoya carnosa* he discovered that half the blossoms on a flower cluster open one night and rest opened the second night. He thought this action was light related but when he placed the plant in a dark cupboard the same thing happened. Thinking the plant's behaviour might be related to a non-visual part of the spectrum such as x-rays he did a further experiment with *Mimosa pudica* or Sensitive plant. The Mimosa would open and close its leaves in a closet the same as it would in the sunlight. To test his theory he took Mimosa plants down 200m into a coal mine and found they would not open because they were shielded from the natural radiation coming from the atmosphere.

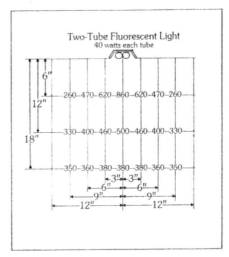

Light intensity in foot candles.

He also found that some plants were very sensitive to electrical fields. When he was filming "On a Clear Day" with Barbara Striesand, the geranium plants that grew very close to the *cathode* at the end of the fluorescent tube were stunted and the roots grew in every direction. When he moved the plants to the centre of the tube their health improved and the roots grew down in a normal fashion. When the cathodes were shielded the plant growth was normal.

Light appears to be so closely connected with cell metabolism, hormone production and photosynthesis that healthy growth cannot take place without the right combination of wave lengths that are found in full spectrum light. There is probably a similar argument that can be made for the impact of light on human performance, e.g., Seasonal Affective Disorder.

Using a combination of cool white and warm white fluorescent tubes will give the widest spectrum and the best results. Some fluorescent tubes are sold as grow lights, but may not produce the full spectrum they claim. Ask for some manufacture's specifications.

Plants and Light

The spring and fall equinoxes are points on the earth's orbit where both hemispheres receive the same amount of sunlight.

From the spring equinox to the summer solstice the days get longer and from the fall equinox to the winter solstice the days get shorter.

In the spring, gardeners look forward to these longer days because it means a new growing season and warmer weather. We have long known that many plants are light-sensitive and react to the increasing day lengths by coming out of dormancy or flowering to produce seed. With some plants, the same reaction can occur when the days shorten.

Plants that respond to decreasing light levels are called "short day plants" and will only start to set flower buds if they have less than twelve hours of light. A shorter day is a signal to the plant that winter is coming and the plant has only a limited time to reproduce. A good example of this type of plant is the chrysanthemum. Colourful potted mums are available for sale year round, only because the growers use blackout curtains in their greenhouses to regulate the number of hours of light. No matter when you buy your potted mum, if you plant it in the garden, it will not start setting buds until the late summer or early fall as the days shorten.

Another short day plant is the Christmas poinsettia. It needs lots of sun during the day but must have about forty nights with thirteen hours of total darkness to trigger the production of showy bracts and tiny blooms. Any interruption of this schedule may prevent the plant from blooming.

When plants respond to increasing light levels they are called "long day plants" and these plants will flower and set seed very quickly as the days lengthen. Many vegetable gardeners have been disappointed when trying to grow spinach. No sooner have the plants come up than the seed heads start to form and the leaves fail to develop. To have success with spinach, seeds must be planted in a cold frame very early in the spring and harvested before the middle of May. Commercial growers also use blackout curtains in the greenhouse to produce spinach all year long. Radish is another long day plant that is prone to go to seed very quickly as the days lengthen.

Most plants are unaffected by *photoperiodism* or day length. Roses are a good example, as they will come into bloom as soon as the weather warms and bloom right through until the frost knocks them back in November or December. In warmer climates, roses are almost non-stop bloomers.

All plants seem to be affected by the need to grow towards light—this is called *phototropism*. The plant produces a hormone called auxin that increases cell production on the dark side of the plant, causing it to bend and grow towards the light. Frequent rotation of potted houseplants that get uneven light exposure will create a more even growth pattern.

Many plants, particularly houseplants, are very sensitive to light intensity. Some need to be up close to windows while others are happy in a lower light area. Ficus benjamina or the 'Benjie Fig' is a classic example of a light-sensitive plant. If you move this plant to a darker location once it has adapted to a particular light intensity, it may react by dropping many of its leaves. In very low light areas, the onset of fall can trigger the same reaction. Plants that are very light sensitive may have to be moved closer to the window in the winter and further back in the summer.

To produce chlorophyll, the green chemical that is so important in photosynthesis, a plant needs the right balance of ultra-violet and infrared light. This is also true for photosynthesis, the process when the plant uses light energy to convert carbon dioxide and water into sugars and starches. A full range of light is available in sunlight but artificial light may be lacking at both ends of the spectrum. Using both a cool white and warm white fluorescent tube will provide a wider range of colour on the light spectrum.

Some seeds also require certain colours of light to germinate. For example, seeds from red impatiens plants will germinate more readily if they have extra blue light. This can be achieved by covering the seed tray with a sheet of clear blue cellophane. Many seeds such as salvia need full light to germinate.

Plants that are subjected to darkness immediately switch from producing sugars, using photosynthesis, to consuming sugars through respiration. Respiration in plants can be slowed down by reducing the temperature while the plant is in the dark.

Understanding plants' needs for light and the various reactions to it, will allow you to have greater success with both your home and garden plants.

CHAPTER SEVEN

Water & Irrigation

Water awareness has become very much a part of the gardener's world in the new millennium. With increasingly warmer weather, rapid urban growth and water infrastructures that are unable to deliver unlimited water supplies, wise use and conservation of water has become extremely important.

Knowing when to water and how much to water is always a puzzle for beginning gardeners. To determine how much water plants are getting from rainfall, a simple rain gauge is a useful tool. You can either purchase a simple, tapered, clear plastic one that is easy to read or use any straight-walled can and a small wooden ruler as a dipstick. Be sure to place the rain gauge out in the open where it is not in the rain shadow of a tree or building. During the winter when the temperature is low and the ground is very moist or frozen, little if any watering needs to be done. One exception may be raised beds under the eaves that receive no rainwater. Winter drought will cause immature flower buds to drop.

The incorrect use of water in the garden can be counter-productive or wasteful. A dry soil surface does not mean the garden needs watering. When the spring daytime temperatures get up to 15° to 18° on a regular basis and the precipitation is less than 2.5 centimeters per week, it is time to start checking the soil moisture. Check the moisture level by scratching away the top 2 or 3 cm of surface soil. If the soil is damp beneath, there is no need to water. However, if the dry soil goes down to the root level of the plants you are growing, then it is advisable to water.

There are two ways of checking the amount of irrigation water applied. One is to set out several straight walled cans and measure the collected water. Two to three cm of water in the can will be adequate for the graden in most instances. The other is to dig into the soil to see how far the irrigation water has penetrated the soil and whether it has reached the old moisture level. The same procedures can be used for natural rainfall. I have found on occasion when planting bulbs in the fall, the soil 15 to 20 cm below the surface is still bone dry in spite of summer irrigation and several heavy fall rains. Deep watering will encourage deeper roots to develop.

Running sprinklers hour after hour is not only a waste of water but will leach valuable nutrients out of the soil and into nearby water courses, contributing to pollution. Once you have measured the amount of time it takes to administer 2–3 cm of water to the garden it is easy to set a time limit for future waterings. It is far better to water once a week at the full rate than twice a week at half the rate. Delivering 2.5 centimeters of water each week to an area will allow it to soak down into the root zone where the water is needed. If the rain gauge shows this amount of natural precipitation then no watering is required. Applying too little water encourages the roots to grow on the surface causing the plant to come under stress during the mid to late summer. Applying too much water may drive out the oxygen and create a waterlogged condition for the plant roots.

Choosing the right time of day to do the watering is also important. Watering in the early morning is by far the best time. Plants have time to absorb moisture before the long hot day begins, the sunshine is not strong enough to cause excess evaporation and leaf surfaces have time to dry during the day. Watering in the evening after the plants have lost some of their turgor through transpiration is not beneficial and plants that go into the night with wet leaves are far more susceptible to mould and fungal diseases. Very cold water will cool the plants and soil for 12 to 15 hours which may slow the growth of heat loving plants. The main problem with midday watering is the excess evaporation that can occur on a hot day. The myth about water droplets on the leaves acting as a magnifying glass is not true. If it was, every leaf in the tropics would be spotted and burned from the midday rainfall and extremely hot sun.

Some plants are far more drought resistant than others. Choosing the right plant for the right place and preparing the soil before or after planting with compost and mulch will help you conserve water, reduce labour and give better results.

Choosing the right kind of sprinkler is very important and having more that one type can be beneficial when trying to water selective spots in the garden. To determine if your sprinkler is effective, set out a half dozen straight walled containers around the extremities and in the centre of the area to be watered. Let the water run for an hour and if the amount of water in the containers varies more than 10% to 15% throw the sprinkler away or take it back to the supplier and tell them it does not work. This exercise will also tell you how many hours it will take to deliver 2.5 centimetres of water to a given area. Anything less is not as effective and anything more is a waste of precious water. Orchard type sprinklers may work well for lawns but they tend to knock down tender annuals and tall perennials

As mentioned in an earlier chapter, the type of soil, organic content and the use of mulch will all have an effect on the retention of water. One way to help conserve water is to cultivate the soil. This helps to slow down the rate of *capillary action* or the soil's ability to pull water to the surface where it more readily evaporates. Do not start cultivating if the soil is still sticky after being watered. To prevent compaction of the moist soil use a short board or piece of plywood to stand on if you have to step off a walkway or path.

In many regions where water shortages have become a regular summer problem, the use of drip irrigation hoses has become popular. You can pull hoses from bed to bed, but the best method if you can afford it is to have permanent soaker hoses running through the beds so that you only have to connect to the main water source. Soaker hoses reduce the amount of evaporation and deliver the water to a very precise area. They also are less inclined to weigh down plants with a heavy layer of water on their leaves.

Installing an automatic irrigation system makes life a whole lot easier for a gardener but is much more expensive. Prices vary from region to region. Laying out an irrigation system can be a fairly technical procedure. Arrange to have several quotes and follow up on the references given to make sure the company you deal with has a good reputation. The cheapest is not always the best.

CHAPTER EIGHT

Temperature & Frost Zones

Plant Hardiness Zones

With the advent of winter weather, gardeners should be aware of plants that need mulching or winter protection. Through years of experience, gardeners and nursery staff have learned which plants will survive in their area. The novice gardener, however, does not always know which new plants will survive.

To standardize the concept of hardiness, horticulturalists have created hardiness zones for the world. Unfortunately, like most systems, people can't agree and several different patterns have been set up. The American and Canadian zoning is slightly different but the zone numbers in our area are essentially the same for both systems. Plant labels on imported plants may cause some confusion so it is best to always check with your nursery.

There are ten zones with 1 the coldest and 10 the warmest. These zones have been worked out, based on average temperatures and plant survival rates, over long periods of time. When using the zones it is wise to remember that they are guidelines, not absolutes, and good judgment and common sense have to be used. Sub-zones are sometimes indicated by using (a) or (b) behind the number. In this case (a) refers to the colder area and (b) to the warmer area of each zone.

Much of the West Coast Marine climate is zone 8 with select areas being 9. The head of fjords or long glaciated inlets are partially moderated by marine air but are also subjected to very cold air pouring out of the continent and are rated as Zone 7. These cold winds can also have an effect on the islands at the mouth of the inlets depending whether you are on the windward or leeward side.

Areas that are more than a hundred kms from the coast area are also Zone 7 but at higher elevatons it is down to Zone 6 or lower.

Below are the hardiness zones.

30-Year Average Winter Lows
1961 – 1990

Zone	Celsius	Farenheit
1	below -45	-50
2	-45 to -37	-50 to -35
3	-37 to -29	-35 to -20
4	-29 to -23	-20 to -10
5	-23 to -20	-10 to -5
6	-20 to -15	-5 to +5
7	-15 to -12	+5 to +10
8	-12 to -7	+10 to +20
9	-7 to -1	+20 to +30
10	-1 to + 5	+30 to +40

Cold hardiness is a very relative term because there are so many variables. Each garden or area within a garden can have its own micro-climate depending on sun exposure, air movement, precipitation and elevation. A sheltered location that receives winter sun may be a few degrees warmer during the day and radiates back some of that heat from the ground at night. House walls can have a similar effect.

Excess rainfall or poor drainage can increase the lethal effects of cold weather on a plant's roots even though, under normal conditions, the same low temperature is not likely to kill the plant. Frequent freezing and thawing can also exaggerate the effects of cold weather, particularly for plants that don't stay dormant.

A heavy frost in early November before plants have had time to harden-off or become covered with a blanket of snow is more damaging than a similar frost in January. Strong, cold winds can often desiccate a plant to the point where it will not recover.

Don't assume that if a plant is hardy in the ground it will also be hardy if planted in a tub, window box or raised planter. Frost is able to penetrate from all sides and roots are generally not as hardy as stalks and branches. Mulching or insulating with straw, ferns, leaves, burlap, styrofoam chips or plastic, can often make a difference.

Plants that can survive freezing temperatures have adapted in many ways. Some have a form of anti-freeze (sugar in the form of raffinose and stachyose) in their cells, while others are able to expand slightly to prevent the cell walls from exploding. Plant scientists are currently trying to splice "frost protecting genes" into some tender crops, such as tomatoes. Plants that are frost hardy and become dormant allow most of their sap to flow down into their roots where the food is stored and excess moisture is expelled. In the spring, with maple trees, for example, the process is reversed. Some plants wait until the very cold weather hits before losing their moisture. This is why rhododendron leaves lose their turgor and droop in cold weather. Trees that retain too much moisture in very cold weather will often explode from ice pressure.

The next time you acquire plants, check the hardiness rating to assist you in knowing where to grow them.

Effects of Frost

Small or self-seeded bulbs that are planted close to the surface may have been heaved out of the ground by frost action. Bulbs that have been exposed or partially heaved should be replanted as quickly as possible before the roots dry out or the bulb becomes sunburned.

As with bulbs, many small perennial plants are also prone to lift during the freezing weather, particularly if they have not been mulched in the fall. If they appear to be sitting too high or are loose, they may require replanting. Frost damage of this type is a good indicator that a winter mulch should be applied next fall.

In areas of the garden where bulbs or plants are growing up through the leaf mulch, it is wise to clear the mulch from new leaves and let them unfold freely. Tightly bunched emerging bulb leaves can lift clumps of soil which should also be removed. With the exception of woodland garden areas where there is a covering of moss, leaf mould or mulch material should be left in place as long as there is a threat of heavy overnight frosts.

Plants are not the only thing that may have been heaved by the frost. Patio or sidewalk bricks will usually settle back in place but wooden edging boards that are secured with stakes won't settle as readily. Using a piece of timber or a sledgehammer, knock the boards back into place before the soil settles in underneath. This may also be necessary around flowerbeds if they are edged with wood, brick or plastic. Mowing the grass where the edging material is too high is a nuisance.

Some tender or marginally hardy plants will no doubt be damaged or lost as a result of a winter's cold snap. Check the stalks and crowns before you cut or remove any plants that appear dead. Using the blade of your clippers, start at the top of each stalk and gently scrape to see if there is any live (green or white) tissue. If it is only brown then keep testing as you move down. Even though all the stalks are dead there may still be life in the crown or root structure and new sucker shoots will develop. An old crown with a good root structure will usually regenerate quicker than a new plant. Don't replace the specimen until the plant has had time to declare itself.

CHAPTER NINE

Pruning & Shearing

O f all the garden practices and procedures, I suspect that pruning is the most misunderstood and poorly done. Lack of knowledge or anxiety about pruning often leads to major mistakes or complete avoidance of the task. Pruning or cutting away wood from a tree or shrub is a long-established necessary practice of gardeners.

Unfortunately some gardeners hate to prune anything, while others become chain saw specialists. In fact many garden plants don't need any regular pruning while others such as hedges might be sheared two or three times a year. Many large trees should never be severely pruned because the growth pattern from then on will look distorted.

Pruning Tools

Before you start pruning, make sure you have the proper tools. For most small gardens a good pair of hand pruners or secateurs and a sharp pruning saw are probably all you need. Long handled loppers are fine if you have a lot of rough slashing work but they tend to bruise the bark on larger branches in the cutting process. A telescopic pole pruner can be useful, but a pair of hand pruners and a ladder will do a far more precise job.

The best type of secateurs to use are the ones that have a very sharp bi-pass blade, similar to scissors. Felco 2 have long been the industry standard. Anvil type shears, where the sharp blade presses against a flat surface will crush or bruise the wood during cutting. A good pair of secateurs should last many decades and are well worth the extra money. Pruning saws are best if they have a folding blade.

Why Prune?

There are a variety of reasons. The first one is to remove all damaged, dead or diseased wood from the plant. This includes branches broken by animals or snow, branches that have died back from frost or lack of light as well as parts of the plant that have become infected with disease which has the potential to spread.

Sometimes the dead wood on a tree or shrub is actually caused by incorrect pruning from a previous year. Branches that are not cut at a junction or a dormant bud will generally die back to the junction or bud and leave what is called a stub. If the diameter of

Example showing results of not removing tree ties and branch stubs on a maple tree.

the tree is growing at a rate of 3 mm/year it will take 8 years or more to grow and callus over a 24 mm stub. In that time, with our wet climate, the stub will rot back into the main trunk and cause bigger problems.

The removal of dead or decaying wood from trees and shrubs is also important. The decay will soon work back into the supporting branch or trunk. When this happens it is difficult to contain the rot without disfiguring the tree or creating a huge wound.

A second reason for pruning is to maintain a desirable form, balance and size for the plant. This, however, does not mean you should try to make a midget out of a giant. The more you cut, the more sucker growth the tree will generate. If the tree cannot be left to grow to its regular size because of space limitations, then it might make more sense to remove the tree or shrub and plant something that is more appropriate for that site. Constant pruning every year in order to keep the plant a certain size creates extra work and may eliminate the bloom. Plants respond best when they are allowed to grow in their natural form rather than shaping them into cones or lollipops. Appropriate pruning will help to maintain form, balance and size.

Plants such as Forsythia and Mock Orange need to be pruned to keep them under control, stimulate new growth and maintain a desirable form. Regular pruning of fruit trees will improve the quality and quantity of fruit by directing more of the energy into fruit and less into woody growth. Old trees can be brought back into production by judicious pruning although it may take a few years to develop new growth and fruit spurs.

Fruit trees, in particular, need regular pruning to maintain satisfactory health and vigor. Too much tight growth will prevent light and air from reaching the inner part of the tree, thereby encouraging dampness, fungus, lichens and disease. When old apple trees have not been pruned for years, they will appear to revert back to a wild state, producing large quantities of small fruit. After a judicious pruning the tree will come back into production with large fruit.

Pruning determines the growth pattern, removes excess non-productive wood and stimulates the production of more fruit. Cutting back the new growth on a mature apple tree to three or four buds each year will trigger the growth of more fruit spurs. These are knobby little appendages along the branch with a fat bud at the end. When the branch is cut the two lower buds will generally produce fruit spurs and the new terminal bud will develop new growth. If the procedure is repeated every year, there should be a good number of fruit spurs and plenty of apples if the weather co-operates to allow the bees to pollinate the blossoms.

Mature wisteria vines are pruned in order to produce more flower spurs and give you a better show of colour in the spring. They are best pruned using a similar method to that of apples, following the three-bud system. (*See page 89.*)

As you can see from the examples given, it is important to know the reasons or objectives of pruning before you make the first cut. You will be more satisfied with the results and the job will become easier each year.

When to Prune

One major concern people have about pruning is timing. The only pruning I do in the late fall is to cut down dead stalks to improve appearance or to prevent snow damage on live plants. The top one third of hybrid roses, hardy fuchsia, some of the clematis varieties and the dead hydrangea blooms are a few that benefit from this late fall pruning. Sometime before Christmas I prune my grapes. If you leave your vines to be pruned until late January or February and there is a mild winter, they have the propensity to bleed and there is no way to stop the flow of sap. Birches and some maples are also prone to bleeding if pruned in late winter or early spring.

Plants that are best pruned in the late winter before the blooming period include hardy hibiscus, hydrangea (both the mop

Pruning Guide for Flowering Shrubs

1. Prune for renewal
3. Shorten branches
5. Do not prune if possible

2. Prune for shape
4. Forms buds the previous year
6. Do not cut into brown wood (will not regenerate)

Species	Time of year	Purpose	Notes
Abelia	early spring	1, 2, 3	bushy form is best
Amelanchier	after flowering	2, 5	keep to 2 m
Aucuba japonica	growing season	2, 3	treat as laurel
Azalea	after flowering	4, 5	
Berberis	after flowering	1, 3, 5	thorns are problem
Buddleia	after flowering	1, 2, 3	prune hard
Callicarpa	early spring	2, 3, 5	
Calycanthus	after flowering	1, 2	remove old wood
Camellia	after flowering	2, 3, 4, 5	
Ceanothus	after flowering	2, 3	
Chaenomales	after flowering	1, 3	blooms on mature wood
Chimonanthus	early spring	2, 3	sprays for winter
Choisya	after flowering	2, 3, 5	semi-hardy
Cornus	after flowering	3, 4, 5	varies with type
Cotinus	early spring	2, 5	
Cotoneaster	early spring	2, 3	almost any time
Cytisus	after flowering	1, 2, 6	prune early
Daphne	after flowering	5	watch for fungus
Deutzia	after flowering	1, 2, 3	needs open space
Elaeagnus	after flowering	2, 6	reverts to green
Enkianthus	after flowering	2, 3, 5	
Erica-calluna	after flowering	2, 6	2.5 to 5 cm of green
Escallonia	after flowering	1, 2, 5	
Euonymus	early spring	2, 3, 5	
Fatsia	early spring	1, 2, 3	vary stalk heights
Forsythia	after flowering	1, 2, 3	
Hamamelis	early spring	2, 3	
Hardy Fuchsia	late fall	1	mulch over winter
Hardy Hibiscus	early spring	2, 3, 5	late to leaf out
Hebe	after flowering	5	half hardy
Hydrangea	early spring	1, 2, 3	3 buds only on P.G.
Hypericum	early spring	1, 3	prune to ground
Ilex	early spring	2, 3	sprays for Xmas
Jasmine (winter)	after flowering		stake and tie
Kalmia	after flowering	2, 3, 5	
Kerria	after flowering	1	
Kolkwitzia	after flowering	1	very large
Laburnum	after flowering	2, 3,5	thin centre growth

Species	Time of year	Purpose	Notes
Lonicera	after flowering	2, 3	prune to 3 buds
Leucothoe	after flowering	1, 2, 3	
Magnolia	after flowering	3, 4, 5, 6	
Mahonia	after flowering	2, 3	
Malus	early spring	2, 3, 4	
Nandina	early spring	1, 2, 5	remove old stalks
Osmanthus	after flowering	2, 3	
Paeonia	early spring	5	remove dead wood
Philadelphus	after flowering	1, 2, 3	very large
Pernettya	early spring	5	
Pieris	after flowering	2, 4, 5	renew old plant
Potentilla	early spring	1, 2, 3	
Prunus	after flowering	2, 3	
Pyracantha	after flowering	1, 2, 5	save blooming wood
Rhododendron	after flowering	4, 5	move if necessary
Ribes	after flowering	2, 5	
Rosa	early spring	1	remove old wood
Rubus	early spring	5	
Skimmia	after flowering	2, 5	
Spiraea	after flowering	1, 2	
Symphoricarpos	early spring	1, 2, 3	
Syringa	after flowering	2, 4, 5	1 for old trunks
Viburnum	after flowering	2, 5	
Weigela	after flowering	1, 2, 5	
Yucca	after flowering	1	remove old rosette

head and the P.G.), potentilla and roses. This group of plants will form bloom on new wood and not as well or not at all on old wood. Hardy fuchsia can be placed in this category but is best pruned in the late fall when the first heavy frost ruins the last of the leaves and flowers. I like to chop up some of the soft woody shoots into 20 - 30 cm lengths and lay them on top of the plant as a mulch to provide additional frost protection.

Most fruit trees except cherries can be pruned any time in late winter before bud break in spring. Flowering shrubs such as rhododendrons and camellias that set buds one summer and bloom the following spring, should be pruned right after flowering. This would include flowering cherries. Shrubs such as roses that develop flower buds on new wood can be pruned before the new growth starts in the spring.

What to Look For

Pruning is always a major job for late winter when the buds on many bushes and shrubs are swelling in preparation for opening. Most garden plants fall into one of two categories when it comes to pruning, those that require pruning before they bloom and those that must be pruned after they bloom. Look at the plant to see if the flower buds have already formed. If so, then hold off on the pruning until after they have bloomed.

On plants such as azalea, camellia, lilac and rhododendron, the buds are generally quite large and easy to see, whereas on Choisya, escallonia, forsythia and kalmia, they look more like a regular growth bud.

When pruning deciduous plants it is essential you know where the dormant buds are. It is best to look for the old leaf node scar because there will always be a bud at the leaf node. To encourage growth pointing away from the centre of the plant, look for a dormant bud that is on the outer or underneath side of the branch. This will allow you to direct the future growth out or down. After several years of careful pruning you can keep the branch growing in the direction you want and help the tree or bush develop an open or candelabra style structure.

When fruit trees are very young the primary purpose for pruning is to develop the basic structure. Four or five years after the fruit tree starts to mature, the reason for pruning is to enhance the flower and fruit production. Branches that put on 30 to 90 cm of growth each year can be pruned back to three or four buds. The last bud should be chosen to direct new growth in the coming season and the other buds will hopefully develop into flower and fruit buds which are called spurs. Over the years the fruit spur will put on new growth and become 12 to 15 cm long. Great care must be taken not to cut or break off these twisted fruit spurs, as they are the basis for next year's fruit crop.

Some vines such as wisteria and grape can be pruned in a similar way to most fruit trees. Once a framework has been developed, the vine can be cut back to three buds, removing three to five meters of new growth. Again, the last bud will create new growth and the other buds will produce growth or flower buds. If the vine is not cut back severely each year all the energy will go into new woody growth with very little left for flowers or fruit. It may take a wisteria five or six years to become established but after that it can become "jungle warfare" if it is not pruned regularly.

When you cut a stem beyond a dormant bud, the distance should be about 1/8" to 3/16" away from the bud. If you cut too close, the new growth may break away from the stem. If you leave a long section beyond the bud, the stub will die and the resulting decay may move back to, or below, the growth bud.

Cuts that are made on upright branches should be made at a slight angle to ensure that drainage will occur. This is particularly true for roses, which have a large area of pith, or soft spongy wood, in the centre of the stem.

When cutting large branches close to the trunk of a tree, look for a collar or slight enlargement as the branch enters the tree trunk.

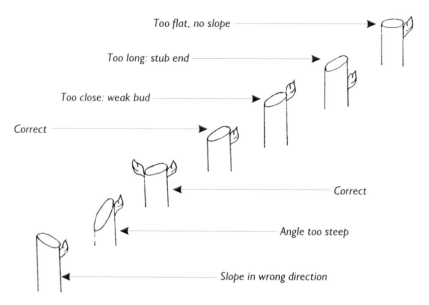

Right and wrong pruning cuts.

When pruning, leave the collar to reduce the scar area. The specialized cells in the collar will allow the wound to callous over much more quickly. The wound should be left untreated because pruning paints and gums will hold moisture in and cause rapid decay.

If a large tree branch is to be removed, it is best to follow a procedure using three cuts. The first cut is placed about 60 cm from the trunk and is started on the underneath side of the branch. When the saw starts to bind, remove it and start the second cut 65 cm. from the trunk on the topside of the branch. The branch should split between the saw cuts and fall free if it has not been secured. The final 65 cm. stub can now be removed with a third cut with no risk of splitting the branch down into the side of the tree trunk. Pre-tie or support heavy branches as a safety measure before any cuts are made.

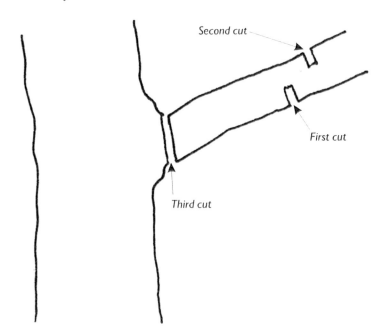

Triple cut for large branches.

Pruning for Renewal

Some flowering bushes and shrubs produce the best blooms on relatively new wood and they must be pruned for renewal. Hydrangeas, peaches and roses are good examples of plants where a portion of the old wood is removed each year to encourage new stalks to emerge from the base of the plant or trunk of the tree. Other shrubs, such as abelia and viburnum, need have only their branches shortened back and a compact shape developed. Azaleas and rhododendrons don't require any pruning under normal conditions. If they get too big it is better to move them and plant some dwarf or semi-dwarf varieties to take their place.

Shaping a plant during the pruning procedure is often done, but many times I see every plant sheared into a ball or "lollipop." Not only is this not the natural shape of the plant, but it also results in a lot of old hard wood that is not producing flowers and may be more susceptible to disease.

Pruning for renewal allows the plant to generate new wood and remain healthy. To renewal prune, one must go to the base of multi-stemmed plants and remove 1/3, 1/4 or 1/5 of the old stalks close to ground level, depending on how vigorous the plant's growth is. If you do this every year, the plant will be on a three, four or five year renewal cycle.

A good example of a plant that needs renewal pruning and only a light shaping is Hydrangea macrophyllum (mophead or lacecap). When the old stalks start to develop a lot of side shoots and the old papery bark begins peeling, stalks should be removed to make room for new growth. The large straight stalks remaining need only have the old bloom cut off down to the first two large opposing buds. In some cases shaping the plant may require you to go down to the second or third set of buds but they will also produce flowers.

Other examples of plants that require renewal pruning before or after blooming would be abelia, chaenomales (also known as quince or japonica), forsythia, kerria, philadelphus (mock orange), potentilla, rose, and spiraea. In a few cases where there is so much growth that it is impossible to get in and thin the stalks it may be necessary to cut everything down and start over again with new sucker shoots.

All established plants develop a ratio between their root structure and top growth. If a plant or tree is severely pruned the ratio is changed and the root structure may now be twice the size it needs to be to support the reduction in top growth. The excess nutrient capacity will usually stimulate rapid top growth until the ratio is brought back into balance again. To prune severely one year and then abandon the tree the next, generates a maze of suckers or water shoots during the following two or three years, often creating a worse problem than if the tree had not been touched. However, there are some plants that are valued for their sucker growth. Red and yellow osier, members of the dogwood family produce excellent winter colour on new growth. In this instance, heavy renewal pruning gives the best results. As soon as the bark on the stem starts to turn grey and loses its colour, the stem should be cut a few centimetres from the ground to encourage new growth and more colourful sucker shoots.

Heather and related plants are often neglected when it comes to pruning. Most varieties bloom in the fall, winter or spring and need to be pruned, or sheared, as soon as the bloom fades and definitely before any new growth begins. Shear off the old flowers, leaving 3 to 5 cms of green growth for new shoots to develop on. The bare brown stems on an old heather plant will not regenerate new growth or blooms and may have to be replanted after 10 or 12 years

Pruning Grafted Trees and Shrubs

It is important to be aware of special problems when pruning grafted trees. Grafting means that parts from two different trees have been spliced together to grow as a single specimen. Most often the root of the tree is different from the trunk and branches.

However, there are some situations where the root, trunk and top branches are from three different plants.

Grafting a new top section onto a different trunk or trunk onto a root may be done for a variety of reasons. For example, the plant may not root readily from cuttings or it takes too long to grow a large plant from seed.

One of the best examples of a double graft is a pendulous or weeping form of Japanese cherry (Prunus subhertella pendula). As the tree matures there will be a slight bulge at the base of the trunk where the trunk was grafted to the root. About two meters up the trunk just below the first whorl of branches there will be another bulge or ridge where the top section was grafted to the

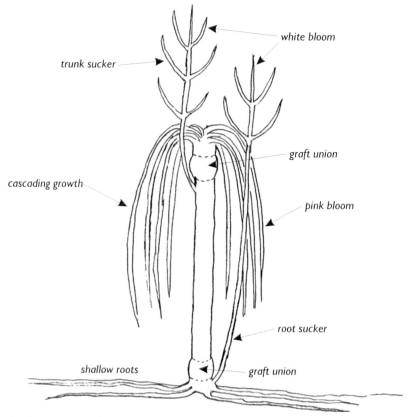

Suckers on a grafted cherry tree.

trunk. Any sucker shoots coming from the base of the tree below the graft will resemble the wild cherry rootstock. Shoots coming from any place on the trunk below the top graft will resemble a sweet cherry. Both types of sucker shoots will probably be more vigorous than the top growth and display none of the weeping character. If left to grow, the sucker shoots will grow up through the weeping branches and ruin the tree's ornamental value.

Weeping Birch (Betula pendula) and Weeping Pussy Willow (Salix caprea pendula) are two other examples of top grafted trees that may form suckers below the graft, overpowering the weeping branches in a relatively short time.

Hybrid roses and certainly most hybrid tea roses are grown on grafted rootstock and have the potential to produce sucker shoots from below the graft. If your rose bush produces flowers with two different colours or leaf patterns you have a sucker shoot that should be pruned out from the rootstock.

All fruit trees are grafted on to special rootstock because they will not come true from seed. Many nurseries use special dwarf rootstock to produce dwarf fruit trees. To meet the needs of the home gardener, fruit trees are now being top grafted using three and four different apple varieties. Pruning off the wrong branch can completely eliminate one apple variety.

The weeping or pendulous forms of maple (Acer palmatum dissectum) are not top grafted but are trained by staking a single leader to the height required before allowing the plant to follow its natural tendency to weep. If you want the tree to grow higher you can stake a new leader and create a new canopy of branches. The only pruning this maple needs is to have the dead wood removed from under the canopy.

Plants will sometimes go through a hereditary change either at the seed stage or, less commonly, at the bud stage. Many of our new plant varieties are created this way. However, some of these genetic mutations are not stable and will revert back to their original form. I have seen single branches on several dwarf Alberta Spruce trees

(Picea glauca albertiana conica) revert back to their non-dwarf White Spruce parent. A similar problem will occur with some of the broad leaf shrubs where the variegated or coloured leaves revert back to regular green. Should this happen, the abnormal branch or leader should be pruned out before the plant loses its value.

CHAPTER TEN

Pests, Diseases
& Other Wildlife

During the main growing season gardeners are faced with a host of problems affecting their plants. These problems can show up as weeds, fungus or pests such as insects, mites and mollusks. In our fast-paced world most gardeners want quick and easy solutions to their problems and have been conditioned by the chemical companies to think that the solutions come in a bottle or can.

In the 1940's with the introduction of the insecticide DDT, the lives of thousands of allied troops in South-east Asia were saved by wiping out the mosquitoes that spread malaria and yellow fever. With such success in the war zone it was not hard to convince North Americans that chemical sprays were the answer to their pest problems in their home gardens and on the farm.

It was not until around 1973 after the publishing of Rachel Carson's "Silent Spring" and some disturbing evidence about the cumulative nature of DDT, that the governments of Canada and the US decided to ban the use of this pesticide. However, they did not ban the right to manufacture the product, meaning it can still be made and shipped to developing countries, some of which produce food for us. As one writer puts it, "The problems of today were the solutions of yesterday."

In spite of the hundreds of chemical sprays that have been

banned over the last three decades, we still have thousands more that have been licensed for farm and garden use. They are tested for oral dosage and dermal exposure but little is known about the interactions and effects of long-term exposure to low-level concentrations. Apparently, it is not uncommon to find traces of twenty to thirty pesticides in still water ponds. In highly developed residential areas there are more pesticides used per hectare of land than on many farms.

The pesticide/herbicide industry is a multi-billion dollar business that produces millions of tons of product each year. Unfortunately, none of the material is retrieved and therefore, has to be dispersed in our environment.

Many garden sprays and chemicals are used in an indiscriminate way. Home gardeners may not be too adept at identifying problems and will use a fungicide when an insecticide is required.

Indiscriminate spraying of everything that crawls or flies may do more damage to beneficial insects than to harmful ones. As the saying goes, when you kill a beneficial insect you inherit its work. Not only do you want to protect beneficial and predatory insects, but you also want to make sure they have enough insects to feed on and survive in your garden.

Instead of rushing out to spray at the first sign of an infestation, it might be wise to wait and monitor the problem. Give the predatory insects a chance to move in and do their job. Ask yourself if it really matters whether there is a small blemish on the rose leaves or a few minor notches in the rhododendron leaves. This brings to mind a comment I heard recently, "When I achieve personal perfection, I will expect it of my plants."

Most garden plants have dozens of different cultivars. By talking to fellow gardeners, checking catalogues and using trial and error methods, you can choose the plants that are the most trouble-free. For example, if you have a rose that is very susceptible to black spot and powdery mildew, it might be better to discard the bush rather than continually spray it. Many of the species rhododendrons and some hybrids, are resistant to weevils because they taste bad.

Well-maintained plants are less susceptible to disease and insect damage. Plants under stress emit xylene gas which seems to attract many insects telling them the plant is weak and in trouble. Using a mulch that will both conserve water and slowly feed the plants will help less drought-tolerant plants survive the summer and protect all plants from frost in the winter.

Learning more about your plants will enable you to make the wise choices that contribute not only to the well-being of your plants, but to the health of the environment which affects us all.

Good Bugs, Bad Bugs

For centuries many people have believed that humans are the dominant species on earth and that other forms of life should be manipulated to benefit humans, or even eliminated. This has been particularly true regarding insects and related species. In fact, in our rush to rid the world of pesky insects, we have often failed to appreciate that many insects are in fact very beneficial.

After WW II when the chemical and pesticide industry really started to develop, many leading agriculturalists and public relations personnel working for chemical companies led us to believe that it was only a matter of time until we would live in an insect-free world. Unfortunately our chemical knowledge was ahead of our ecological knowledge and a potential disaster awaited us around the corner.

The general population, and home gardeners in particular, are slowly coming to the realization that not all insects are bad and pesticides are not the foolproof solution we were led to believe.

The Generation X gardeners of today were raised in an era when it was popular to think that if anything crawled, wiggled or fluttered in the home or garden it should be crushed and killed. Nobody wanted creepy crawly creatures touching them or invading their space. The attitude at that time was "the only good bug was a dead bug." This attitude was often passed on to children.

This common approach to insects generally resulted from a lack of scientific knowledge and an inability to determine good bugs from bad bugs within a vast array of creatures. The insect world is so large and prolific that if it were not for some bugs eating other bugs the world would soon be knee deep in insects or insect skeletons.

Even the list of names we have for insects and related species is sometimes confusing. Ranging in size from less than 1mm to 10 cm, some of the beneficial ones are midges, flies, thrips, lacewings, beetles, spiders, bees, wasps, hornets, mantis and centipedes. The problem bugs for our gardens are often more numerous and include mites, aphids, thrips, weevils, beetles, larva, maggots, moths, leafhoppers, leafrollers, leafminers, whitefly, spittle bugs, wire worms, cutworms, cabbageworms, hornworms, caterpillars, scale and earwigs.

Children can be fascinated by insects and other small creatures if taught from an early age that not all creepy crawlies are bad and should be eliminated. One of the best nature walks I ever went on with my own children was with an entomologist who took us on a short walk where he turned over leaves, rocks and small logs to show the group what was hiding underneath. He also taught the children to put the rock or log back the way they found it to preserve the creature's habitat. If more children are raised to appreciate the importance of bugs and other micro life, we will soon have a whole new generation that won't make the mistakes about bugs we did. The difficulty is knowing what is good and what is bad. A greater knowledge of what insects are living in your garden will give you a better idea of how to respond to them.

IPM

The issue of pesticides and their use has recently been a topic for talk shows, newspapers and television news broadcasts. Several local municipalities are moving towards regulating the use of pesticides in the next few years and the courts have upheld their right to do this. Municipal governments might implement restrictions on using pesticides on municipal lands or they could extend the ban to commercial use or even to individual home-owners.

All products promoted or sold as a pesticide must be licensed by the Federal Government under the Pesticide Act. They have recently begun to overhaul the system and update the Act by requiring re-testing of older products and new rules for register-ing new ones. Some of the more commonly used pesticides will probably be taken off the market.

For the average home gardener, it must be a bewildering expe-rience to walk into the pesticide section of a major garden centre. The multitude of products available is overwhelming. The pesti-cide product spectrum runs from the mildest organic material to the most toxic chemical. Many retail garden store employees have their pesticide dispenser's certificate but their knowledge of plant problems and the correct product to apply is not always accurate, in my opinion.

In some cases, home gardeners incorrectly diagnose their plant problems and don't ask for advice when buying pesticides. An example of this is when a Camellia shrub has leaf scale which releases the sap from the underside of the leaf. The sweet sap sprays down on the leaves below and a black mould or fungus grows on the leaf surface. Far too many gardeners rush out and buy a fungicide to treat the problem when it is actually an insect problem and a fungicide doesn't work. Other times gardeners will treat a small infestation of aphids with a strong insecticide when a high-pressure stream of cold water will solve the prob-lem. Also, once the leaf ages and the surface cells harden up, the aphids will cease to be interested and will disappear.

Gardeners seem to be divided into three categories when it comes to using pesticides; those that like to spray everything, those that would like to use pesticides responsibly and only when absolutely necessary and those that don't want to use any sprays at all.

Some twenty years ago some people in the agriculture industry as well as commercial horticulturists, realized the need for more responsible management of pests. They set up a program called Integrated Pest Management (IPM) which was designed to suppress insect populations in an effective, economical and environmentally sound way. Over the last ten to fifteen years the concept has been extended to other problems such as weeds, plant diseases and harmful nematodes. The concept is based on the management and control of pest populations, not the elimination of them.

The key components of an IPM program are:

- Preventing pest problems from occurring by growing the right plant in the right place and encouraging the use of good cultural practices.

- Creating an environment for birds, beneficial insects and natural predators.

- Learning how to identify the problem so that the treatment can be tailored to the particular species or pest.

- Monitoring the pest populations and environmental conditions.

- Determining what level of injury or damage is tolerable or acceptable.

- Deciding what action or treatment is required based on the other components.

- Applying the treatment or control which may be either biological, physical, mechanical, cultural or chemical.

- Evaluating the pest management program and determining how effective it has been.

Sectors of the industry that have adopted an IPM program have reduced their use of pesticides by 60 % to 80 %. If more gardeners adopted an IPM approach the use of pesticides would not be such a serious environmental issue.

Garden Enemy No. 1: Slugs and Snails

The cool, damp climate of the Pacific Northwest is a mixed blessing. It makes our gardens productive and green all year round but is the perfect habitat for two of the most troublesome garden pests we have. Slugs and snails can cause more damage to plants in a few days than almost any other garden pest.

Snails and their evolutionary younger relatives slugs, who lost their calcareous shells along the evolutionary path, belong to the mollusk family. The salt-water members of the same family, such as clams, mussels, octopus, oysters, and squid, are all considered to be delicacies. The golf ball sized garden snails are highly valued by the French as escargot. Maybe if we could eat our snails they wouldn't be considered such a pest.

Slugs and snails do not have a skeleton. They are able to move using a large "foot" attached to a powerful muscle that allows them to pull themselves along a nearly frictionless slime trail. The slime can also protect the soft body from things as sharp as broken glass and razor blades. Slugs use the slime as a glue to cling to vertical surfaces. They can also use the slime trail to track down a mate or find their way back to a familiar hiding place.

The slime may well act as a form of self-defense because many predators find the slime has a bad taste and swells when exposed to moisture or saliva. The slime can actually absorb water from the air to keep the slug's body from dehydrating. Should you get slime on your hands it is best to roll it off like dry glue balls before washing.

Slugs and snails cannot stand dryness or extreme temperatures. Snails can retreat into their shells and create a slime plug, providing the temperature remains moderate. Slugs must find a cool damp hiding place in the organic debris or soil before they dehydrate or freeze. They will generally go to the closest hiding place when the sun comes up and this makes them easier to trap.

Creatures that have both sex organs are called hermaphrodites and slugs and snails fall into this category. When two slugs or snails fertilize each other they both lay clusters of eggs in protected areas or in the soil below the frost line. The eggs are clear and about 2 mm in diameter. Finding and destroying these egg masses in the fall will prevent many problems in the spring.

There are many varieties of slugs and snails and most have been imported on plants or visitors from Europe. Our best-known native slug is *Ariolimax columbianis* or Banana Slug. They can grow up to 20 cm, crawl 10 to 12 m a night and consume 30 - 40 times their weight in vegetation each night. Fortunately, they prefer a forest setting and are not often found in gardens. Our most common slug, *Limax maximus* or Great Slug from Europe, is not as big as the Banana Slug but can move at twice the speed or about 25 cm per minute. The word slug comes from the old Norse word "slugga" meaning slow.

Slugs eat different foods depending on the variety. Some are carnivorous while others tend to prefer humus and fungi. Most garden slugs and snails will eat green vegetation, flowers and fruit. Their mouths are at the base of their heads and the radula or tongue-like structure has hundreds or even thousands of rasp like teeth that scrape the organic tissue away. This allows them to cut into the leaf surface at any point and not just on the edge like weevils or most cut worms. This characteristic is worth knowing when trying to diagnose what is causing leaf damage.

Snails and slugs have some natural predators. Beetles, frogs, snakes, voles and birds will all help to reduce the population. Domestic ducks are particularly good at cleaning up infestations of slugs but they may generate some other problems.

Setting up natural hiding places for slugs and then trapping them is the easiest way to deal with them. Lay a board between rows of plants and then turn it over every other day to catch the hiding slugs. Some gardeners prefer to drown them in jars of stale beer or a bread yeast liquid. Cabbage leaves left in strategic places will also attract them for an evening meal and a place to hide. Slug hunts (with a can of salt) are best carried out in the early morning, late evening or just after a rain.

Traditional slug bait consists of rolled grain soaked in metaldehyde. This is best placed in a coffee can (with plastic lid) that has holes punched in the sides at the base. The can protects the poison from the rain, pets and children. Safer's has a new product out that consists of ferric phosphate granules which is lethal to mollusks but will not harm birds or pets. Any unused bait is degradable and becomes part of the soil

Birds In Your Garden

In winter many birds have exhausted much of their natural food supply and would welcome a handout from local gardeners. Filling a bird feeder for your feathered friends can be enjoyable for you as well as beneficial for them. Indoor winter days become more interesting when you have a variety of bird species close by to observe. Getting to know their names, feeding habits and characteristics is a popular hobby for many gardeners.

Birds, through instinct, will maintain a diet that is well balanced between carbohydrates and protein. Seeds in a feeder will be balanced with the large number of insects, larvae and insect eggs that can be found in and around most gardens. Having the birds working for you by cleaning up your garden will greatly reduce next summer's bug population.

When it comes to feeding, not all birds can be treated in the same way. It is important to know your birds and the type of seeds they prefer. There is no point in buying bird feed that will go to waste or fail to attract a wide range of species. Check the information on the bird feed package or the store where you purchase it.

The location of the feeder is also important. Some birds are ground feeders and are more comfortable standing on the ground or on a raised box to eat. Others prefer to eat from a feeder if their feet are well adapted to clinging.

Some gardens are ideal habitats for birds because they have all the right requirements. Birds need a plentiful supply of natural food and access to water and roosting sites. Choosing the right plants for a bird-friendly garden will improve the general quality of the habitat. Birds need evergreens for winter shelter, multi-branched trees and shrubs for quick protection and nesting as well as lots of berry, nectar or seed producing plants for food.

Some birds such as the Rufus Hummingbird time their arrival back from southern climes by the flowering cycle of the Red Currant and Salmonberry, usually in mid March. If these plants are present in your garden the hummers can be encouraged to stick around for the summer, providing a feeder is set up as soon as they arrive. Once they take up residence, they will sample all the other nectar bearing plants in the garden as they come into bloom. The nectar they consume is a supplement to all the protein they eat. Feeders should be filled with a 1: 4 ratio of sugar boiled in water. Change the solution frequently if the hummers are not feeding. Hummingbirds can be beneficial in reducing the number of mosquitoes in an area.

There is more to keeping a bird feeder than just hanging it and adding food from time to time. Feeders need to be kept dry and cleaned regularly to remove dirt and moldy seed. This will reduce the potential for the spread of disease.

Ground feeding birds prefer a low, covered platform that will not allow predators to ambush them. A circle of chicken wire a short distance out from the feeder may provide the protection they need. The area around the feeder should be raked clean to remove moldy seeds and discourage rodents. Moving a ground feeding station to a new location every few months prevents a build-up of bird droppings and the potential for disease.

Suspended bird feeders are best placed within a few metres of a good perching tree. This allows birds to fly back and forth to the feeder without feeling the stress of long-term exposure.

Birdbaths are a nice feature in the garden if there is no natural water source. The water, however, must be kept fresh and the bath cleaned frequently. Use a 10% bleach solution to wash and sterilize the empty birdbath, and rinse it well before refilling.

Most common bird diseases cannot be contracted by humans. One exception is salmonella bacteria, which can be passed on. Take care to wash your hands after cleaning or handling your bird feeder. Removing dead birds from the garden should also be done with care. Disease is the third most common cause of death in birds after window strikes and cats.

Bird watching is second only to gardening as the most popular hobby in Canada. To get started with this activity or learn more, go to www.wbu.com

Where Have All the Butterflies Gone?

I remember times in the past when you could watch numerous butterflies dancing around the garden during the summer. Now it seems rare to see these lovely creatures fluttering from blossom to blossom.

There are many reasons why butterflies are less numerous today. The widespread use of pesticides, including the so-called organic ones, is probably one of the main reasons for their decline. Farmers and homeowners are much more conscientious about spraying or eliminating weeds along the edge of their property. These weeds may be a good food source for butterflies. Municipalities also tend to mow the roadside verges, which reduces both food and habitat.

Gardeners often ask themselves how they can have butterflies without having caterpillars eating their plants. The fact is most garden caterpillars turn into moths not butterflies. One exception to this rule is the "Cabbage White" butterfly, which lays its eggs on any plant in the cabbage family.

Both the 5 butterfly families and the 75 moth families belong to the Lepidoptera genus. However, there are some distinct differences between the groups. Butterfly bodies are generally slimmer without hair. The antennae on a butterfly are longer and have a swelling or knob at the end. Butterfly wings, particularly those of males, are generally very colourful whereas moths have earth tones. The butterfly rests with its wings in a vertical position while the moth keeps its wings in a horizontal position. The moth does most of its flying at night while the butterfly needs daylight and the sun's warmth to fly. The larva stage of a moth is a cocoon and a butterfly is a chrysalis.

Butterflies and moths are very particular where they lay their eggs as the newly-hatched caterpillars only feed on very specific host plants. Most of our garden plants are not host plants for butterflies but they may be for certain moths. When newly-laid eggs of butterflies hatch, caterpillars eat their fill and then pupate to produce a chrysalis that is encased and hangs from a leaf on silken fibres. The silk worm is a good example of this phenomenon. When the new adult butterfly emerges from the chrysalis stage it begins feeding on nectar to gain strength to breed and lay eggs for the next generation. Like bees, butterflies are good pollinators.

A few species don't feed but simply breed, lay their eggs and die. Some hibernate for the winter as a chrysalis or as an adult in leaf litter. Others like the Monarch migrate to Mexico for the winter and return in the Spring to lay their eggs and complete their life cycle.

Butterflies are real sun lovers and need long hot summers for ideal breeding conditions. Several cool damp summers will greatly reduce their numbers. When they do not have temperatures of 30°C or more they will land on a black rock or dark surface to allow their wings to absorb heat. The black spots on their wings also help them become active.

If you want to see more butterflies in your garden, here are a few things you can do. Butterflies need shelter in the form of small trees or large shrubs to protect them from wind and rain. They need a breeding ground and a rearing site such as a green belt or grassy ditch area that may be adjacent to or close by your garden. This rearing area needs the right host plants for the caterpillars to feed on. Some examples of plants that are a good food source for butterfly caterpillars are alfalfa, poplar leaves, clover, elm leaves, many of the grasses and sedges, nettles, parsley, vetch and willow leaves.

Creating a puddle or placing a saucer of water in the garden for moisture and a flat black rock for heat will attract butterflies.

Adult butterflies need the right flowers to supply a continuous source of nectar from late spring to early fall. The following plants are good nectar sources: annuals: ageratum, marigold, heliotrope, lantana, petunia and verbena; perennials: aster, aubretia, coreopsis, echinacea, eupatorium, liatris, monardna, phlox, rudbeckia, sedum, solidago, sunflower and yarrow; shrubs: caryopteris, buddleia, lonicera, syringa and ligustrum, to name just a few.

By avoiding the use of pesticides and herbicides and creating the conditions necessary for a good habitat you may be surprised how many butterflies show up in your garden

Dogs and Lawns

The popularity of dogs has increased dramatically in the last few years. This has created a variety of problems for their owners and neighbours, particularly if they have lawns. Dog urine and feces can be a frustrating problem when it comes to lawn maintenance. Of the two, urine creates the most damage. It is the amount and strength of the urine that will determine the degree of damage.

The damage to grass and shrubs by dog urine and feces is

related to the concentration of nitrogen. Urine and feces are waste products that remove excess nitrogen from the kidneys and intestine. The nitrogen results from the breakdown of protein in the dog's diet. An excessively rich protein diet will create more nitrogen in their waste.

A small amount of dog urine will create a green patch while a large amount will cause a dead spot generally surrounded with a bright green ring of rich growth. The outer green ring forms where the urine has been diluted and acts as a fertilizer.

Feces are less of a problem for burning grass but have their own set of problems when left on the lawn. If the feces is picked up immediately before it has time to dissolve or leach out the nitrogen, burning will not occur. Removing feces from the lawn also reduces the risk of contaminating children. Apart from soiling shoes and clothes, dog feces may be infected with such things as round worms, hook worms and salmonella. These parasites and bacteria can be picked up by children playing in contaminated areas.

Contrary to popular belief, urine from female dogs does not vary in strength nor its ability to burn. All puppies and females squat to urinate so the nitrogen is concentrated in one spot and causes burning. Male dogs usually learn after approximately a year to lift their leg and deposit urine on a post, bush or rock, which helps to disperse the concentration of urine and do less burning. However, if they use the same spot repeatedly the burning will occur on the shrub or grass at the base of the post or rock.

Male dogs often use their urine as a way of marking a spot, which attracts other dogs to do the same. A boulevard lawn may have 5 to 10 dogs per day visit the site creating an extremely high concentration of nitrogen on a well-scented shrub.

Certain grass species are more prone to urine or nitrogen burning than others. Unfortunately, most of the grass species we grow are the least resistant to burning. In tests done on common lawn grasses it was shown that the concentration of urine was more damaging than the volume.

Knowing the problem is one thing, solving the problem is another. Building fences, picking up feces and advising neighbours about leash by-laws may help protect your lawn, but what about your own dog?

Few dog owners realize that dogs can be trained to use a litter box or designated area in the garden where they can eliminate their nitrogen-rich wastes and stop damaging the grass or fouling the lawn area. The litter area must have a suitable base such as gravel or wood chips that will allow good drainage. Providing a suitable post, large rock or faux hydrant will make the site more appealing to male dogs. Scenting the area with the dog's own urine and feces will make the training easier.

Taking the dog to the site on a leash and rewarding it with food for using the site will establish a pattern of behaviour. Consistency over a two or three week period with a puppy may be enough, whereas with an older dog it may take a month or two. Some dog owners have found it helpful to develop an elimination command as well.

Repairing the damage done to a lawn by dog urine can be accomplished in several ways. Diluting the urine with three times the volume of water soon after it happens is fine if you see the dog urinating. If the burn has already occurred, add water and then scratch the soil surface to create a seedbed. Cover the seed with a dusting of soil and the patch should be green again within 14 to 21 days. A third method is to cut out the damaged sod to a depth of 3 to 5 cm (1-2") and insert a new section of lawn sod. This is the quickest way to repair the lawn. Cutting sections of turf from the edges of your own lawn to use as patches will ensure you have the same type of grass and that you don't have a quiltwork of different coloured grasses.

CHAPTER ELEVEN

Roses

The rose has been valued as a domestic garden plant since the time of the ancient Greeks. In the old English estate garden there was always a rose garden for show and for a ready supply of cut blooms for the house. Small cottage gardens often had a variety of easily cared for shrub roses, as well as climbers or ramblers.

Gardeners today have a wide selection of rose bushes to choose from such as hybrid teas, floribundas, polyanthas, climbers, ramblers and shrub roses.

Planting Roses

Most rose growers plant their new stock in the fall but home gardeners generally find new rose bushes for sale in the garden centers in the spring. If the spring season brings on the urge to plant new rose bushes or replace old ones, a few simple planting procedures will help to ensure healthy plants and greater enjoyment.

Roses prefer full sun and a place of their own to grow. They are heavy feeders and do not like competition from the deep roots of other invasive plants or trees. Some of the old-fashioned climbers or ramblers are less demanding, but will generally do better if they do not have to compete for space or food. Once established, roses do not like to be moved. In the right location roses will grow and bloom for decades. It is therefore essential that the new bush be planted in the best soil possible.

Remember that the various types of roses such as hybrid teas, floribundas and shrub roses can vary in height from 1 m to 3 m. Plants of varying heights may not look good in the same rose garden.

After choosing an appropriate site, plan the placement of the roses so they will be at least 65 to 90 cm apart. This prevents crowding and allows room for pruning and spraying.

When replacing plants, it is wise to lay down a large piece of plastic on which to set the soil and surrounding perennials when preparing the bed. This reduces the clean up time when the job is finished.

Plants with bare roots benefit from being soaked in sloppy wet peat overnight and potted plants should be well watered prior to planting. Peat or paper maché pots should be removed before planting. Begin by digging a hole 45 cm by 45 cm and at least 30 cm deep, removing the soil, rocks and roots. Screen if necessary.

To improve the soil before planting, mix the native soil with two parts of soil and one part compost or aged manure in a wheelbarrow or on a plastic sheet. Add a handful or two of coarse bone meal and dolomite lime to improve the planting mix.

Using the new planting mix, build a mound on which to set the rose bush in the bottom of the hole. Prune any broken or dead roots from the bush and fan out the remaining roots down over the mound of well-packed new soil.

The height of the rose bush crown is critical because it cannot be adjusted after planting. Lay a stick across the hole to determine the ground level and plant the graft union (large lump on the stem) about 2 to 3 cm above ground level. Fill the hole with the remaining soil up to the graft union and tamp firmly. The extra 2 to 3 cm allows for settling of the soil as the plant is watered and the organic material decays. The colder the climate the deeper the bud union can be planted

For winter protection, the graft union can be covered with mulch but should be exposed during the growing season. Cut the canes back to 25 to 30 cm. Climbers and ramblers should be trained on a fence, trellis or wall as the canes begin to grow. The closer the tip of the cane is to the ground the more likely blooms will form on secondary shoots.

Rose Care

Spring pruning should begin when the first new shoots appear or pop through the wax coating that is traditionally applied to new bushes. The timing is usually about a month before the last spring frost. Hybrid teas and floribundas are best shaped into a candela-

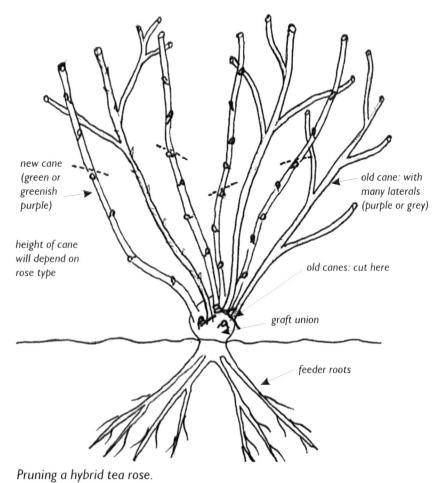

new cane (green or greenish purple)

old cane: with many laterals (purple or grey)

height of cane will depend on rose type

old canes: cut here

graft union

feeder roots

Pruning a hybrid tea rose.

bra form to give each cane room to grow. Always cut above an out-side bud to encourage new shoots to grow away from the centre of the plant. I often use my thumb to rub off buds or shoots that are growing in the wrong direction or where there are multiple buds coming from the same node. The length of cane after pruning will depend on the type and size of the rose but will be between 25 cm and 1m. Many species and old roses are best pruned after bloom-ing to allow the wood to mature for next season.

Rose pruning should continue through much of the growing season as part of the dead-heading process. Removing old blooms redirects energy from seeds to new flowers. Cut the cane back to the first leaf with five petals or where the cane is strong enough to support a new flush of blooms. Pruning actually stimulates new growth. Once the roses have gone semi-dormant but before the snow comes, it is advisable to shear off the top one third of the hybrids and floribundas to prevent them from suffering from snow damage. The final pruning is then done in the spring.

Roses have deep roots and need to be well watered during the growing season. Mulching not only helps to hold moisture but will also provide nutrients, weed control and frost protection.

The first application of fertilizer (approximately 2.4.5 ratio) should be applied shortly after the canes produce some signifi-cant buds. By the time the fertilizer dissolves and reaches the roots, the plant will be ready for it. Some rose growers give each plant a quarter cup of magnesium sulphate (Epsom Salts) to give the plant a boost in the spring and correct any magnesium defi-ciency. Additional lime may be required to keep the pH between 6 and 7. A second application of fertilizer should be applied after the first flush of blooms has finished around mid-July. These two fertilizer applications can be supplemented with a medium handful of slow-release fertilizer for each plant, placed just under the soil or mulch where it will remain warm and moist. The fertil-izer pellets need to be wet and above 20°C for the fertilizer to be released over a 90 day period. Do not give your plants any more nitrogen after the end of July and no further feeding after the end

Rose before pruning.

Rose after pruning.

of August. Stop fertilizing and let rosehips start to form to signal the plant to harden off and prepare for winter.

An early spring clean-up is essential for healthy roses. Remove all leaves, spent flowers and portions of cane that may be lying in the rose bed. If any green leaves have survived on the canes during a mild winter, they should also be removed. This will greatly reduce the carryover of disease from one year to the next. You may also wish to spray the rose canes and soil with fungicide-like lime sulphur but this should be done before the new buds emerge. A simple fungicide that can be used during the growing season can be prepared from 4 teaspoons of baking soda, 1 tablespoon of dormant horticultural oil and 4 litres of water. Spray both sides of the leaves and the ground.

Over the years many gardeners have told me about a unique rose they have that produces flowers of two colours. They are often disappointed when I show them that one rose is coming off the stem below the graft and one is coming off above the graft. The other clue is the fact that the lower one has leaves with seven petals whereas the top one has only five petals. The sucker shoot coming from below the graft is off a hardy type of rootstock which is generally Rosa canina.

Maintaining healthy roses can be a fair amount of work, particularly in our damp climate. With proper care, however, your roses will provide pleasure for many years.

CHAPTER TWELVE

Lawns

Lawns are probably the most common feature of most gardens. They require a higher level of maintenance over a longer period than any other part of the garden. Some gardeners are coming to the conclusion that a ground cover does not have to mean turf grass and they are looking for alternatives. (*See Groundcovers.*)

Before you go to work on your patch of grass in the spring, try to decide what purpose your grass is serving and how it will be used. If the area is a place for young children to play and the dog to run, then a coarse, tough grass with a few weeds might be sufficient for the next few years. Other gardeners may want something that approximates a bowling or golf green but this level of maintenance may require professional help. If, however, your lawn is for general use you should be able to achieve your goal without too much difficulty.

Lawn Repair and Renovation

Over the years most lawns will develop slight depressions due to decaying organic material or general settling. If the hollows are not more than 2 to 3 cm deep, the quickest solution is to add an equivalent amount of top dressing soil to the lawn. When top dressing the entire lawn, you can drag a plank or ladder over the dressing to remove the high spots.

If, however, the lawn has major depressions, a thick layer of top dressing will only substitute one problem for another. Before trying to eliminate the depressions, you should first determine why they are there. Using a piece of reinforcing steel or an iron bar, poke a hole in the low spot to see if there is a partially collapsed septic tank or grease pit below. In other cases a large depression may be an old stump hole that was filled with debris and is now decaying. It may take 2 or 3 m³ of mineral or sub-soil to fill these potentially dangerous holes.

Adding six or seven inches of top soil to a deeper depression will only make the grass grow much faster and create bright green humps instead of hollows. It is better to repair the depression by cutting the turf in twelve-inch strips and rolling it back like a jellyroll. Scrape off the thin layer of exposed topsoil and add enough mineral soil to the hole to level the mineral base. Replace the topsoil and roll the turf back into place. This procedure keeps the turf, top soil and mineral soil at a uniform depth and the growth rate of the grass the same.

Another problem area for lawns occurs with trees, such as flowering cherries, which are prone to develop a few very large surface roots when planted in poor soil. If you cut the roots, the tree will be deprived of nutrients or be more susceptible to root rot or blowing over. A series of top dressings will slowly raise the soil level enough that your mower blade will go over the roots without scalping them. Burying the roots too deep will also cause problems.

In areas where small patches of grass have died or trees or bushes have been removed and you want to restore the grass, it is wise to use some of your own turf to fill in the space. Go around the edges of the lawn where the grass has been creeping into the beds or over the walks and slice off enough thin strips to patch the bare spot. Fill the cracks between the strips with top soil and in two or three weeks you will hardly know a repair job has been done. This turf patching procedure can also be used very effectively when redesigning the shape of lawns and beds. The turf that is lifted in one area is used to replant in another, providing the total area of lawn is the same or smaller.

Using new grass seed to patch areas of dead grass creates the risk of having a permanent yellow-green grass showing up as a patch in a blue-green lawn or vice versa.

Any new seed that is used should be the same as that of the original lawn and be feathered well out into the old lawn so there is no definite line between old and new lawn composed of different grasses. To do this effectively, bare patches and turf areas must be top dressed lightly to allow good seed germination well out into the old lawn.

Over time most lawns will develop colonies of weed grass that will gradually overtake the lawn grass. These weed grasses show up because they are lighter or darker in colour, have wider grass blades, are faster growing and may form seed heads. When the lawn is full of weeds, weed grass or moss and the soil level has sunk well below the sidewalk, it might be time to consider rebuilding the lawn. There is no point in adding topsoil to this weed patch and planting new grass because the existing weed grass will come back up through the soil.

Killing the grass and weeds can be accomplished in several ways. The quickest way is to spray a non-selective herbicide such as Roundup on the grass and wait two weeks for the grass to yellow and die. Be sure to water the lawn and germinate all the dormant weed seeds and then spray a second time. You do not want your new lawn infected with the same weed grass killed with the first spray. Roundup has low toxicity and is quick to break down in the soil.

A second way is to purposely burn the grass by spraying it with a very strong solution of urea fertilizer (46.0.0). This must be done on a dry day when you expect three or four days of nice weather. The residual fertilizer will be used by your new turf or partially absorbed in the composted grass.

The most organic method is one that can be used only in areas of full sun during the summer months. Cover the grass for one to two weeks with clear plastic and seal it at the edges with boards or soil allowing the solar heat to pasteurize the soil and kill the grass and weeds.

For all three methods of killing, the dead grass and weeds must be raked or scraped off before putting down a new layer of topsoil, grass seed or sod. A layer of organic debris below the new soil will prevent the movement of moisture both up and down.

Some people prefer to use sod which is about ten times more expensive than grass seed, but it does produce an instant lawn. Beware that sod can easily be destroyed by your neighbourhood raccoons before it takes root and becomes a lawn.

A thin layer of sod planted on top of a gravel or clay base is the most difficult situation to remedy. To add successive layers of top dressing over the years may make the lawn higher than the sidewalks and may cause bark rot on buried tree trunks. If you have to correct the situation, it is best to lift the sod using a sod cutter and bring in a machine to lower the grade by 10 to 15 cm, so topsoil can be added before the turf is re-laid. This is a costly procedure, which would not be necessary if care had been taken to plant the lawn properly in the first place.

Lawn Care

The first step in caring for your lawn is to deal with that perennial problem of moss. Shade, dampness and poor soil all contribute to a healthy crop of moss. In areas of heavy shade and low traffic it might make more sense to mow the moss and learn to live with it, or switch to a suitable ground cover.

There are several ways to kill moss but all of them require extra work each spring. An economical way to do that is to share the rental fee with a neighbour for a Mantis power rake and each of you can do your lawn. The machine will also rip out the thatch and some of the creeping weeds. However, if the grass is weak or thin the power rake will rip out everything. A second method is to use a special moss rake and cancel your classes at the gym. Using a power mower and grass bag is a quicker and more effective way to pick up loose moss than using a grass rake.

Any residual moss that is left can be killed with moss killer. Moss killer can be applied like a fertilizer to a damp or wet lawn when you expect there will be two or three days of dry weather. Another method is to dissolve iron sulphate in very hot water and spray it on a dry lawn at the beginning of a dry period. To avoid plugging the nozzle, do not mix the iron sulphate in the sprayer. The spraying must cover all areas or you will have a zebra striped lawn. The sulphate kills the moss and the iron acts as a tonic for anemic grass.

When disposing of moss, it is important that you do not place more than 1 to 2 cm of dead moss in the compost box at any one time as it does not decompose readily.

Lawns that have not been well maintained will often build up a layer of thatch or dead grass. If the lawn feels spongy when you walk on it, you have a thatch and/or moss problem.

Many soils are naturally very acidic because of high rainfall and the possible use of sulphur coated fertilizers. Grass prefers a soil with a pH of 6.5 so an annual application of dolomite lime at 20 kgs /97 m² is recommended. Do not apply the lime before removing the moss as you may rake out much of the lime with the damp moss.

At least one week after the lime has been applied and the grass has started to show signs of growth, it is time to fertilize. The two should not be applied together as the lime helps to free up the nitrogen too quickly. Good lawns need to be fertilized three to four times a year. Use a slow release fertilizer with a ratio of 3.1.2. The middle number represents phosphorous and is the least likely to leach out of the soil. Frequency of use will depend on the type of fertilizer applied. A cheap, quick release fertilizer will promote a rapid flush of growth and the need to mow the grass twice a week.

More people are opting to go with an organic fertilizer as opposed to a straight chemical formulation. Organic fertilizers have the added benefit of additional microbial activity and a slow release rate.

Mowing is an important part of lawn maintenance. Start the season by cutting the grass very short to remove the old or dead grass. This can be done before power raking. As the new grass emerges raise the mower and allow the grass blades to reach approximately 4 to 6 cm. Each time you mow you should not be taking off more than 1/3 of the new growth. Removing only a third of the grass blade at each mowing will help maintain colour and prevent a yellow stubble from forming. This may mean you will have to mow the grass more than once a week if it is growing rapidly. Grass clippings can be left on the lawn during the dry season. They will break down and provide extra fertilizer.

The shorter the grass blade the less sun energy can be converted into food reserves and the less root structure will be available to draw nutrients. Longer grass during the hot dry season will also help to delay your lawn from turning brown so quickly. Raise the blade a notch when hot weather arrives.

Weeds are always a problem and can sometimes take over a lawn. Some people use a weed and feed type fertilizer but this is an indiscriminate use of a toxic chemical. If chemicals are required to get the problem under control it might be better to buy a very small amount of weed killer and selectively spray those areas that need treatment. Mix half the amount of weed killer that you think you need because there is no place to dispose of the leftover liquid. Remember to dress appropriately, wear gloves and follow the directions on the label when you are applying a spray. Do not add the first batch of grass clippings to the compost. Once the grass is reasonably free of weeds it is far better to weed by hand, removing a few weeds each time you walk across the lawn. Grass that grows tall, is lighter in colour or goes to seed very quickly is weed grass which is difficult to eradicate. Pull out the colonies by hand before they become too large. There is no selective spray for weed grass.

Lawns that are subject to very heavy traffic should be aerated. A coring machine can be rented for this purpose or a lawn maintenance person hired to do the job. Rake the cores off and make compost out of them or leave them to dry and break them up with a rotary mower.

Many lawns have been planted in very poor soil and over time the organic matter disappears. Check your soil for quality, depth and drainage. To do this, cut out a soil core and see what you have for a base. Plan to add a high quality compost based top dressing if there is less than 10 cm (4") of soil. This provides nutrients, microbial life, and a new root area. Commercial gardeners usually top dress in conjunction with coring and/or reseeding.

Lawns perform best when they get about 2.5 cm of water a week during the growing season. Frequent but shallow watering encourages a weak root structure. (*See Irrigation page 76.*)

Remember the time you spend on your lawn in the early season will pay great dividends by the time you want to sit outside and enjoy it.

Lawn Diseases

Poorly maintained lawns are far more susceptible to diseases. Most lawn diseases are caused by fungus or insects. The three most common insects to feed on grass roots are: grey grubs or leather jackets (crane flies), and white grubs (European chaffer and white lawn moth). In most cases a healthy lawn will not be severely damaged by these pests. A third less common problem is ant nests in the lawn. They are not visible until the grass starts to yellow from lack of moisture due to the many subterranean tunnels. Put out some bait (2 parts washing borax and 1 part icing sugar) as soon as you see the problem.

Fungal diseases are more common and becoming more of a problem. In the early spring, particularly if it is wet, problems can be caused by algae, Fusarium Patch and Pink Snow Mold. The roots and crowns are not affected and the grass will generally come back. Avoid high nitrogen fertilizers in the fall and don't leave the grass blades too long over the winter.

During the spring and fall, Fairy Rings, Leaf Spot and Melting Out are common. Fairy Rings are circles of dead grass up to 15 metres in diameter adjacent to dark green grass. Mushrooms often appear in the rings. They are difficult to control. Keep the turf well fertilized and maintained.

Leaf Spot and Melting Out show up as purplish red spots on the grass blades. In severe cases the whole plant will turn reddish brown and then die.

Fungal diseases that are common in the summer are Take All Patch, Red Thread and Rust, which is more common in the late summer. Take All Patch starts as a brown circular depression that slowly increases in size. As the circle increases, weeds and weed grass colonize the centre creating a doughnut pattern. Red Thread is showing up more frequently on many lawns and can be identified by its irregular patches of discoloured grass. On the ends of the grass blades there will be very fine red fibres protruding from the blades. Rust is most prevalent on blue grasses and shows up as yellow or brown spots which can cause the entire lawn to go yellow in severe situations.

Newly planted lawns are also susceptible to fungal diseases. If the grass seed fails to emerge or the new seedlings turn yellow and collapse it could be caused by Damp Off, a group of fungal diseases such as pythium or fusarium.

There are many different fungicides on the market as remedies for fungal diseases. Before applying one, check with your local garden store or nursery to see which one is recommended by the Ministry of Agriculture, Food and Fisheries.

CHAPTER 13

Bulbs &
Bulb-Like Plants

Gardeners refer to almost anything that is thick, fleshy and planted underground as a bulb. The word bulb is used as a generic term. To get the best results from this family of underground plants known as *"geophytes"* you have to know their category or sub-category and how hardy they are. Two things all geophytes have in common are underground buds that sprout under the right conditions, and the ability to store food.

True bulbs are defined as plants with swollen underground leaf tissue growing out of a basil plate that supports roots. True bulbs can be divided into two sub-categories: tunicate and scaly bulbs.

Tunicate Bulbs

When the outer swollen leaf tissue or leaves die on a bulb, it forms a tough skin or tunic-like protective coating around the bulb. When the bulb is dried, the tunic becomes a distinctive papery covering. A few examples of a tunicate bulbs would be allium (onion), daffodil, hyacinth and tulip.

Contrary to popular belief, the tulip did not originate in Holland but is native to regions of Turkey and Iran. These areas have a Mediterranean climate to which tunicate bulbs are well adapted. When you check the origin of most tunicate bulbs you will find they originated in the same climate zone. Mediterranean climate is also an ideal area to grow grapes and produce high-quality wine. Think of your major wine producing areas such as the Mediterranean region, South Africa, Western Australia, Chile and California and you will have identified the home of most of the tunicate bulbs.

Tunicate bulbs perform far better if you are able to approximate the general climatic conditions to which they are accustomed. A typical Mediterranean climate area has cool, damp winters and long, hot, dry summers. Bulbs planted in the fall will start to develop roots when the temperature drops below 16°C , usually around mid-September. They will also take advantage of the fall and winter rains to develop a good root structure. The bulbs will be ready to sprout leaves and support a flower stalk in the spring as soon as the soil warms. This cooling process is called *vernalization* and it is essential for all fall-planted bulbs. Once the leaves die back in the spring, the bulb lies dormant and insulated in the warm dry soil until the cycle begins again the next year.

Unfortunately, most bulb growing areas have cool or cold winters where the soil is either very wet or close to freezing. The summers are also moderately wet and most garden soils are kept moist by irrigation during the summer to support annuals, perennials, shrubs and trees. After a few years of excess summer moisture many tunicate bulbs lose their vigour and become infected with fungal diseases and subsequently die. The obvious question is how do the commercial growers get around this problem? They grow their bulbs in well-drained soil without irrigation and allow them to fully mature before digging. The bulbs are then stored in a cool dry place for the summer, duplicating the dryness of a Mediterranean summer. If the bulbs are not up to market size they are replanted in the fall and grown for another year.

Home gardeners have several options. Tunicate bulbs can be planted under deciduous trees where they will get early spring sunshine and the tree's root structure will guarantee the soil is quite dry during the summer dormant period. A second option is to choose a site with excellent drainage that is on a steep slope, raised rockery or berm. The third option is that bulbs are allowed to mature, then dug up, washed and stored for the summer in a cool dry place. Digging all my tunicate bulbs, particularly tulips, each year is too much work, so I try to lift them on a two-year cycle, which seems to help restore their vigour and health.

Scaly Bulbs

These bulbs have the typical swollen leaf tissue but the bulb is composed of segmented or scale-like sections. They do not have tunics and do not like to be dried at anytime during their life cycle. The most common example of a scaly bulb is a lily.

Most scaly bulbs originated in cool damp climates, such as West Coast Marine, and prefer damp soil during their dormant period. It is interesting to note that tunicate bulbs are sold dry in paper bags while scaly bulbs are sold in plastic bags with damp shavings or peat to help them retain some residual moisture. Scaly bulbs should also be lifted every three or four years, not for the purpose of drying them out and restoring their health, but to break up the clump of new offset bulbs and renew the soil.

Corms

A corm is a swollen stem base, the best examples being found on crocus, gladiola and crocosmia. After flowering, the energy from the old corm moves up into the stem and a new corm forms above the old one. Additional small cormels may form to the side of the new corm and can be grown to form flowering size corms. The old corm gradually withers away and detaches itself. When digging corms it is best to twist off and discard the remains of the old corm. Many corms have a tunic which should be left in place when drying or replanting.

Stem Tubers

A thick fleshy tuber forms at the base of the stem. Examples of stem tubers would be anemone, potato and tuberous begonia.

Each stem tuber may have several "eyes" out of which new sprouts will emerge. Prior to planting potatoes, the tuber can be cut into several sections ensuring that each section has at least one eye. The same can be done with begonias, but the cut surface will not produce new roots so this can reduce the vigour of the plant. The eyes should be on the top surface of the tuber when planting and can be found on the concave or rough surface of the begonia tuber. Potato tubers, unlike begonias, die away after the new tubers form.

Root Tubers
In this case the fleshy tuber is a swelling of the root. Examples of root tubers are dahlias, eranthus and ranunculis. Root tubers have eyes at the base of the stem and will not grow if there are no eyes attached. Before splitting root tubers it is often necessary to pre-sprout them in a tray of damp peat to determine where the eyes are at the base of the stem.

Rhizomes
A large fleshy root that continues to grow and divide into segments. The best examples of rhizomes are canna lilies and bearded iris. Some rhizomes such as the canna lily prefer to be planted below the soil surface while most bearded iris require one third of the rhizome to be exposed.

Growing Bulbs

Over the years I have found it is much easier to grow small bulbs that need little care and are easy to naturalize. It is easy to plant a small number of bulbs using several varieties. Let them grow and multiply by seed or off sets and enjoy the colourful show for several months each spring. They require minimum care. In seasonal order a few examples would be eranthis (Winter Aconite), galanthus (Snow Drops), crocus, chionodoxa (Glory Of The

Snow), Muscari (Grape Hyacinth), puschkinia and brodiea. There are hundreds of other spring and summer bulb-like plants you can grow depending on your growing conditions, garden design and particular interests.

Crocus

There are at least twenty members of the crocus family with *Crocus vernus* or one of its many hybrids being the common spring crocus. When the crocus blooms, it sends up a long thin flower stock with a *stigma* at the top. When the stigma is pollinated the pollen has to travel all the way back down the inside of the stalk to the bulb where it fertilizes the ovules. As the ovules form seeds the seed capsule grows back up to the surface and eventually releases the new seeds. This is why it takes several weeks from the time the flower is pollinated until the seed capsule appears above the ground. Let the seeds disperse or collect them and plant them in a new site. It takes a long time for the new crocus corms to develop and this will not happen if the crocus leaves are cut off before they start to turn yellow. Planting the corms close to a sidewalk allows you to avoid digging them up when preparing a bed for other plants. It also allows you to flip the crocus leaves out of the bed when planting annuals and then back onto the bed to mature. Never tie bulb leaves in knots as this cuts off the sunlight and prevents any further development.

Crocus sativus is not a common garden variety but it is widely grown in Mediterranean countries as a commercial crop for its stigmas. The stigmas are hand picked from the newly opened flowers and then dried, ground and sold as saffron. Powdered calendula petals are sometimes passed off as a cheap substitute.

The autumn or fall crocus, *Colchicum autumnale*, is not a true crocus. It has the peculiar habit of growing leaves in the spring and then producing large pink, mauve or white flowers in the early fall. The plant is programmed to respond to cooler weather and shorter days and will bloom in the garden shop bulb bin if not planted on time. Most parts of the colchicum plant including the corm are poisonous which makes them a good plant to grow if you want to deter deer or squirrels.

Hyacinth
No other spring bulb produces the strong scent of a hyacinth flower. Driving through a 50-hectare field of these blooms can be almost overpowering. They are best planted close to a well-used walkway or under a bedroom window where the perfume can be enjoyed for the short time they are in bloom. Hyacinth bulbs are one of the only bulbs that have different coloured tunics. The purple or white tunic will indicate at which end of the spectrum the flower colour is.

Iris
Most iris have rhizomes but there are some that produce tunicate bulbs. Both bulbs and rhizomes can be planted in the fall. Late August or early September is the best time to lift rhizomes to renew the soil or transplant. The top of the rhizome should be flush with the soil surface when first planted and one third exposed after the rain compacts the soil.

Lily
There is a wide selection of lily species to choose from and most have highly scented flowers. They will grow in a wide variety of soils and conditions but prefer a rich well-drained soil that is cool and damp. A general rule is to keep their heads in the sun and their feet in the shade. Seeds or bulbils that form in the leaf axils will root on the surface and pull themselves down to the depth they prefer.

Narcissus
There was a day when all daffodil flowers were in the yellow range of the colour spectrum and flowered on a single stalk. Now you can buy daffodils that are pink or may have three flowers to a stalk. There are 13 divisions or classes of daffodils based on their

form. As a flower, daffodils look great in the spring sunshine but the foliage takes a long time to mature and die. This can hold up the planting of summer annuals. One way to get around this problem is to plant your narcissus bulbs in large pots and bury them in the ground over the winter. Rather than burying the bulb pots I find it easier to mound up fern mulch around and between the planted pots and cover them with a sheet of plastic to prevent the fertilizer from leaching out over the winter. It is important to leave 1 to 2 cm. of space at the top of the pot because once the daffodil leaves come up you cannot scrape soil away from their base without having the leaves fall over. For a good show, pack your bulbs shoulder to shoulder with a third of the soil on the top and two thirds below. Add bulb fertilizer (3.15.6) to the soil mix before planting.

Pots are lifted and washed in the early spring when the plants begin to show their first leaves. Plain pots can be slipped into larger more attractive containers to provide a splash of colour on your porch or deck. With two boards and four bricks I build a sloping display area for 10 to 15 pots that gives a banked effect visible from the kitchen window. When the blooms are finished I remove the seed heads and return the bulb pots to a less visible spot at the back of the garden where they can be fertilized (liquid 15.30.15) and allowed to mature. You have the option of covering the pots with *Remay* or you can knock the bulbs out of the pot when the leaves start to die back before the Narcissus Fly maggots have a chance to do any significant damage. Check the basil plate for a borehole or squeeze the bulb to make sure it is very firm. Using this method of growing daffodils does not hold up the planting of annuals and the daffodil bulbs (tunicate) are dry and in storage for the summer.

Tulips

A recent commercial bulb catalogue lists 15 different classes of tulip bulbs with hundreds of varieties listed under the various classes. Some are listed as species bulbs (found in nature) while the majority are hybrids. The bulbs are categorized according to form and blooming times: early season, mid season and late season. A general rule is that species tulips with their short flower stalks are early season bloomers and are better able to withstand late snowfalls and heavy rain. The taller the flower stalks on hybrids, the later they bloom. Remember to deadhead tulips as soon as the flower starts to fall apart. This allows all the energy to go into the bulb instead of the seed.

Planting and Harvesting Bulbs

Spring blooming bulbs are planted in the fall and summer blooming bulbs are planted in the spring. Some summer blooming bulbs benefit from being planted in pots or flats in the early spring in a heated area to give them an early start. The bulbs are then transplanted to the garden bed when the weather warms. Use a balanced planting mixture of peat, perlite and sand that will allow easy extraction when it comes time to transplant. Corms such as acidanthera and gladiola respond to this treatment. If you stagger the planting times the blooming period can be extended. A similar thing can be done for dahlias. Place the clump of tubers in a waxed produce box full of damp peat and pre-sprout them several weeks before planting. This will make it easier to split up the clump of dahlias with a sprout on each tuber. When the new sprouts are 12 to 15 cm high they may be removed and used as cuttings to produce new plants. These forced shoots on the newly planted dahlias will also be above ground ready to take advantage of the warm sunshine. Other bulbs, such as fall crocus, are planted in the fall or spring and do not bloom until the fall. Tender bulbs such as amaryllis are planted in the house in the late fall and bloom in the winter. When planting hybrid bulbs, look for the biggest bulbs. Species bulbs on the other hand are generally smaller but will still produce flowers.

The old rule of thumb about planting bulbs to a depth of three times their height is a good guideline for average-sized bulbs, although I have found many bulbs find their own level if left in the ground for a few years. This is certainly true when they start from seed or bulbils on the surface. Bulbs seem to produce more offsets when planted at a shallower depth. Most bulbs do not like wet feet and need a rich well drained soil with a pH of around 6.5.

If you wish to add compost or manure, it must be worked into the soil thoroughly before planting because bulbs do not respond well when sitting in wet, soggy organic compost or fresh manure. Bulbs need more phosphorous and potassium than nitrogen and this can be supplied by organic fertilizers or a granular 3.15.6 or 4.10.10.formulation. Apply at a rate of 5 lb. / 100 sq. ft., working it into the bed before planting or adding it to the planting trench along with lime and working it into the soil. An additional application of a high nitrogen fertilizer at a rate of 1lb / 100 sq. ft. just as the bulb leaves break the ground will give them an extra boost. Do not let the fertilizer fall into the leaf axils as it will burn the leaves. Bone meal (2.14.0) is not a balanced fertilizer and is very slow acting. It will provide very little nutrient to the bulbs in the first year when it is most needed.

Bulbs can be planted in two different ways. A bulb planter is a tapered pipe-like structure with a handle. When you push it into the soft ground it will pull out a core of soil leaving room to plant one large bulb. If you have 400 bulbs to plant you obviously have to pull 400 plugs of soil. The other way is to dig a trench to the proper depth and plant a hundred or more bulbs at a time. Mark the planted trench with sticks to show where the new bulbs are located. There is nothing more upsetting than starting on your second parallel trench and slicing through the large bulbs you have just planted. If you forget to plant your bulbs in the fall it is better to plant them in the winter or very early spring than trying to hold them over until the next season. After a year in storage most bulbs will be wizened and no longer viable.

Lifting bulbs to dry them out or renewing the soil should be done as soon as the foliage starts to die back. There does not appear to be an easy way to lift bulbs. I start at one side of the bed and dig a trench slightly deeper than the bulbs. This allows me to get a shovel or trowel under the bulbs before lifting and shaking away the soil. As I work across the bed I accumulate a pile of soil behind me so I am less likely to slice through any of the bulbs. It is important to retrieve all the bulbs, particularly if you plan to plant a new variety or different colour the following year. Once the bulbs are dug they should be washed, labeled and laid out in the shade in trays to dry. When fully dried, twist off any remaining leaves or old corms and check the bulbs for insects and disease. Plastic trays or flats are good for storage but they need small sticks placed between them when stacked to ensure good air movement. For small numbers of bulbs I use brown paper lunch bags that are left open at the top, placing up to eight bags to a flat. If you are short of shelving and would rather hang your bulbs try using old panty hose or mesh bags. Remember, never store tunicate bulbs in plastic bags where they sweat and mould.

Forcing Bulbs

This has become a common practice both for tender winter flowering bulbs such as paperwhites and amaryllis and many of the common spring bulbs. Unlike other spring bulbs, paperwhites and amaryllis do not need a cool treatment. Hyacinths are one of the easiest and most rewarding spring bulbs to force. Choose three large hyacinth bulbs and place them in a 6″ bulb pot (shallower than a normal pot) so that one quarter of the bulb is above the soil level. The soil should be of good quality and fortified with a teaspoon of bulb fertilizer. Leave 1-2 cm of freeboard on the pot for watering. To prevent the bulb from freezing place it in a 10″ deep trench near the house foundation or some other protected spot. Mark the pot with a stake so you know its location when the trench is filled. Bulbs typically need 12 to 15 weeks for the roots to form, so count backwards from the time you want the bulbs to bloom. The longer you leave the bulbs in the soil, the taller the bulb shoots will be. Wash off the excess soil when you dig the pot and place it in a bright, cool frost-free area for a few days to allow the chlorophyll to form in the young leaves and the flower bud to emerge. Keep the bulb pot in a cool, very bright location for best results. Setting the pot out in a cool frost-free porch each night will extend the life of the flowers. Forced bulbs use a lot of water while growing in the house.

When the flower is finished, cut the stalk out and set the pot outside in a protected area if the weather is not freezing. Continue to water and feed with a dilute solution of fertilizer. Plant the bulb in the garden the following year but do not attempt to force the bulb two years in a row.

You can also force bulbs in window boxes if you have a frost-free place to store the boxes during the vernalization process. I have a double set of window boxes which allows me to move the bulbs out of the way when they have finished blooming. I can then plant up the other box with summer annuals. Bulbs in unprotected containers cannot withstand heavy frost. Setting the bulb container in a large waxed cardboard produce box and filling it with Styrofoam chips may give you the extra protection you need in a mild climate.

Bulb Diseases

True bulbs and bulb-like plants are susceptible to a number of diseases and pests. They usually fall into three categories: fungus, insects and animals. Using good cultural practices will generally reduce the number of problems.

Grey Mould (Botrytis)
This is a common fungal problem that infects many plants and covers the leaves with a grey fuzzy mould. Cool wet weather is ideal for infection and rapid growth. If you are having trouble

with this fungus, treat it with one of the low toxicity fungicides such as copper or sulphur before the infection becomes advanced.

Powdery Mildew

Another common fungal problem consisting of many different species that are plant specific. The white dust on the leaves usually shows up in the later part of the summer when the days are hot, the nights are cool and the leaves are covered with morning condensation. Rainy weather actually helps prevent powdery mildew by washing the spores off the leaves. Treat with copper or sulphur or spray with a mixture of 5 ml of baking soda and 10 ml of light dormant oil in a litre of water.

Fusarium

A large group of fungi that cause bulb and root rot by plugging up the plant's circulatory system. The spores persist in the ground for several years and there is no simple treatment for the disease. Storing damp or improperly cured bulbs will help spread the fungus.

Aphids

There are thousands of different species of aphids and some attack bulbs. Aphids suck the sap from new growth (immature leaves and stems) causing damage to the plant tissue, spreading viruses and weakening the plant. There are many chemical and organic sprays available to control aphids but I find the simplest way is wash them off with a strong spray of water. Regular monitoring and watching for the presence of ants will help prevent the aphid colonies from getting out of control.

Narcissus Bulb Fly

This bumblebee-sized fly attacks a variety of true bulbs including snowdrops, hyacinth, tulips and amaryllis. The adult fly lays eggs at the base of the plant and the newly hatched maggots work their way down to the basil plate where they bore up into the bulb. The core of the bulb including next year's embryonic flower is then eaten. The maggot is grey and can reach 2 cm in length. Flies are active from mid-May to the end of June and can be prevented from laying eggs by covering the bulb foliage with *Remay cloth* or digging the bulbs before the maggots can do significant damage. Check the basil plate for holes and the bulb for firmness. When in doubt cut a bulb in half to check for the maggot's presence.

Moles
These small furry rodents do not eat bulbs but create tunnels through the bulb beds in search of worms. Their activity disrupts and damages the bulbs in the process. Mole traps or chicken wire cages seem to be the only thing that stops the damage they do.

Squirrels
Grey squirrels, a non-native species, are one of the most destructive rodents in the garden. They might be better called bushy-tailed rats. Laying fine chicken wire or hardware cloth just below the soil surface in newly planted bulb beds will prevent rodents from digging and eating the bulbs. It does not prevent them from pulling up the bulbs once the leaves emerge. Containers and window boxes filled with bulbs are prone to damage. I use a live trap to get rid of them altogether but, like rats, new ones continue to move into the garden.

CHAPTER FOURTEEN

Vegetables

There are a great many reasons why vegetable gardens are coming back into vogue. It might be an interest in growing organic vegetables, the joy of picking super crisp, fresh green peas and having readily available salad greens and tomatoes or the excitement of growing a pumpkin for children. Whatever the reason, it is rewarding to have a small patch of ground for growing vegetables.

Choosing a Site

Choosing the site is important for success. Most long season vegetables require a minimum of six hours of midday sunlight (9 am to 3 pm) between the spring and fall equinox, March 21 to September 21. If you are only growing radish that take 30 days to mature, the long period of sunlight is not as important. Trees or other obstacles that block the sun for an hour or two may require you to have additional morning and afternoon sun.

Avoid sites that have overhanging trees as this restricts available light and rainwater. Tree roots will quickly invade the improved soil in a vegetable garden. If roots are a problem, consider using a root barrier. Any 10 mil plastic or corrugated fiberglass panel placed vertically in a 50 cm ditch will generally block most roots.

Most west coast soils are shallow and deficient in both nutrients and organic material. Plan on double digging (two shovel depths) to remove all rocks, roots and weeds before amending the soil with generous quantities of compost or manure.

Most homeowners do not think of a vegetable garden as part of their landscaping but with the new colourful greens and interesting vegetables a well-tended vegetable garden can be an attractive part of a home garden. Some gardeners who are short of space actually mix their flowers and vegetables in the same bed, taking advantage of gaps and bare spots to tuck in a head of lettuce or a tomato plant.

Choosing Plants and Seeds

For the beginning gardener it is sometimes difficult to decide what are the best vegetables to plant. Ask yourself the following questions:

- What is the site and soil suitable for?
- What are some of the easiest vegetables to grow?
- What will compete with store vegetables when it comes to freshness and price?
- What surplus vegetables can be stored, canned or frozen?
- What vegetables do you really like?

Ordering a few good seed catalogues six months before planting time will give you some useful information and help you make choices about flavour, yield and characteristics. Seed catalogues also have a wealth of information about starting dates, germination temperatures, seeding depths and maturation times. Look for a local, national and heritage type catalogue for comparison of varieties, availability and price.

A common mistake when planting is sowing all your seeds at one time. This may be fine for some crops but having twenty-five heads of lettuce all maturing the same week is not a good use of space. Stagger the plantings based on what you can use at any given time.

To conserve space, some items can be interplanted or double cropped. Radish matures in 30 days and parsnips will take 150 days, so if they are both planted in the same bed, the radish will break the soil for the parsnip seedlings and be harvested long before the parsnips are ready. Spinach must be planted very early in the spring to prevent bolting because it is light-sensitive and will mature about the time tomatoes should be planted in mid-May. The same ground can therefore be used for both crops.

Spacing and positioning each plant is important. In some cases this can be achieved by thinning or pulling out the excess seedlings to make room for the mature plants. In other cases with transplants, one has to anticipate what space the mature plant requires. Be sure to place the short plants on the south or sunny side of the bed and the tall ones on the north or opposite side. You do not want the corn stalks shading the carrots.

Caring for Your Vegetable Garden

Compost and manure will enrich the soil, but additional fertilizer is often required to get the best results. Be sure you know if the vegetables are leaf, seed or root crops and then use the appropriate fertilizer. 4.10.10 is a good all-purpose fertilizer for many vegetables. Fertilizer can be worked into the soil before planting or added as a side dressing mid way through the growing season.

Soil in a vegetable garden should be kept constantly moist but not water logged. Some root crops such as radish and carrots will not fill out quickly if the soil is too dry. Scratch the surface to check the moisture level and cultivate to help conserve moisture and remove competing weeds. Add 2.5 cm of water each time you water and try to irrigate in the morning so the plants will have time to dry during the day. The plants and soil are cool in the morning and cold water will be less of a shock to them. Overnight dampness tends to encourage mildew, particularly on peas.

A number of plants will need staking which is best done as soon as the plants are up and growing. I have found that installing 2 m tomato stakes with strings tied on the stakes at 30 cm intervals as soon as the new indeterminate plants are set in place saves time later and reduces the risk of plants falling over and snapping off. If I notice a tomato that needs tying it is just a matter of walking over and tying it. I do not have to go looking for the string and scissors or putting off the task and regretting it the next day when the plant breaks in an overnight rain. For determinate tomatoes, I use four shorter stakes and run string around the plant to hold the multiple stems in place. Tomato cages can be used for small cherry type tomatoes but I find them too small for most bush type tomatoes.

Fish net and chicken wire work well for supporting beans, cucumbers and peas. Bamboo poles in the form of a teepee work well for pole beans. Cucumber, squash and pumpkins grow well if they are allowed to tumble down over a sunny bank or rock wall, even though it is not part of the vegetable garden. Large rock outcroppings will act as a heat sink and release warmth during the night, which many squash-like plants love.

Raised Vegetable Beds

For many of today's urban dwellers the vegetable garden is something that is associated with a past era. My own memories bring back images of long rows of beans, beets or carrots that took forever to weed and cultivate.

Before my time, when it was necessary to grow enough vegetables to sustain a large family over the winter, the work involved often required the assistance of a horse for plowing and cultivating. Vegetable rows were long and widely spaced to accommodate a horse. Long after the horse was no longer used the garden layout persisted, more through tradition than necessity.

Most modern vegetable gardens are smaller, more productive and involve far less work than they did a century ago. Today most astute gardeners use an old world system of raised beds and block planting. Not only does this system use less space but a given area can be far more productive with less labour. Raised beds also provide better drainage and allow the soil to warm more quickly in the spring.

It is best to choose a site that has full sun for at least six hours during mid-day. It should be well drained and not likely to be invaded by roots from large trees.

The sides of the raised bed can be constructed from any durable material such as cedar boards, planks, concrete blocks or landscape ties. The height of the bed can vary from 10 to 30 cm or more. The deeper the bed the greater the range of vegetables you can grow.

Placing a cap or frame on the top edge of the bed will make the bed look more attractive and provide a useful area to sit on when working. This takes the weight off your knees and strain off your back.

The width of the bed should be customized to your arm length. Half the bed width should be equal to the distance from your shoulder to your wrist. This means you never have to step into the bed to do any work. Compaction is eliminated and wide pathways become unnecessary.

The length of the bed will vary depending on the required size of the vegetable garden or your level of enthusiasm. The best procedure is to set up three raised beds two to three metres long in an area where you have room for expansion. If a small bed proves to be inadequate the first year, the length of each bed can be extended until there is sufficient space. Starting small and achieving success is better than taking on too much in the first year.

Creating three beds has several advantages. In the first bed grow those plants which produce edible leaves such as lettuce, spinach and Swiss chard. In the second, try some plants that produce seeds such as peas, beans and corn. This leaves the third bed for the root crops of carrots, radish, turnips and parsnips. Each group of plants creates different fertilizer demands on the soil. Leaf crops will demand more nitrogen, whereas seed and root crops will require more phosphorous and potassium. Rotating the crops in the beds in subsequent years will give each section of soil a rest. The other major benefit of a three-bed rotation system is the avoidance of disease and insects. By moving the plants each year they are less likely to be reinfected by soil borne larvae or fungus.

Raised beds always require more soil than what you have in the garden. One method of gaining extra soil is to sink the raised bed into the existing top soil and then dig the path areas down to the same level and add the soil to the bed. By sinking the frame 7.5 cm into the soil and then using the path soil to add to the bed you might gain 15 cm of soil. Add 5 cm of backyard or commercial compost to this soil and you will have a bed 20 cm deep. As you add more organic material to the soil each year it won't take long to build up a depth of 35 cm of rich soil.

Be sure to screen or hand pick all the rocks and roots from the existing soil because many vegetables, particularly root crops,

1.2 x 2.4 m. (4' x 8') Raised Vegetable Beds

Rotate crops each year

leaf crops → seed crops → root crops

low plants   high plants

add shaving or sawdust

path soil

compost
path soil
original soil   mixing these 3 layers will provide a good base for beds

have tap roots that do not like rocks in their path. Rocks can also be hard on tools and fingers when working in the soil.

Aligning the beds in a north-south direction may not be possible, but it is the preferred way. This arrangement allows morning sun on one side, midday sun from above and afternoon sun on the other side. To improve the solar exposure, plant the short crops at the south end of the beds and the tall ones at the north end.

With a limited space for planting you may wish to construct cold frames to fit over the raised beds. This will allow an early start and a double crop from the same ground. If the raised beds and portable cold frames are all the same size they will be interchangeable from year to year.

By planting your raised beds in blocks rather than rows you not only save space but you leave little room for weeds to grow. For example, a .6 m by 1.3 m bed would allow you to plant fifteen heads of lettuce or several hundred carrots. Before planting perishable vegetables such as lettuce try to anticipate what your weekly needs might be. Other crops such as carrots can be used or hilled up for late fall or winter use. Creating a camber on the soil surface for each bed and then covering it with clear plastic during the winter prevents the rain from leaching nutrients. In the late winter or early spring sunshine will heat the soil slightly above air temperature encouraging worm activity and germination of weed seeds. With a little easy weeding you will start the season off with weed-free raised beds.

If you have never grown vegetables, it may be time to try a new type of vegetable garden in a raised bed and have the pleasure of harvesting a bountiful crop.

Veggies in Containers

In a recent study done in the US, 69% of the home gardeners questioned said they enjoyed growing their own fruits, vegetables and herbs because it gave them a feeling of personal satisfaction.

Contrary to traditional thinking, you don't need a double lot or a huge backyard to grow a little produce to give you this same feeling. With the increase in urban living, more people are growing plants on patios or balconies.

Growing vegetables in containers is really not that much different to growing them in the ground. Think of the containers as being just a more compact growing area. You will definitely have to do a little more planning, as well as choose your plants carefully, being very particular about maintenance. A plant in a container is a plant in captivity which cannot fend for itself.

Choosing a sunny location is paramount. Fruits, vegetables and herbs all require five to six hours of mid-day sunshine to grow properly. With this much bright sunlight during the summer, plants will need a good supply of moisture to hold them through the heat of the day. Pot saucers, trays, soil with a high organic content and water holding polymers will all help to conserve water.

Except for root crops, most vegetables and herbs can be grown in relatively shallow pots. The wider the pot, the more plants that can be grown. If your containers do not have drainage holes, drill several holes and add some gravel or small pebbles to the bottom of the container. The gravel will be of little use unless you cover it with horticultural fabric to prevent the soil from filtering down into the gravel and blocking the holes.

Placing small pieces of wood or decorative feet under large containers will allow drainage trays to be slipped underneath. For smaller containers, supports will prevent staining or decay on the deck surface.

Plastic and ceramic containers hold moisture better than wood and terracotta. Wood and plastic are much lighter to move around or rotate for more light.

Fill the container with a good quality, lightweight potting soil, or mix your own by using 4 parts garden soil, 3 parts compost (steer manure or other organic amender) 3 parts peat and 2 parts perlite.

Many common herbs are cold hardy and can be kept in pots

over the winter if given a minimum of protection. Others, such as basil, need to be planted each year and then discarded in the fall when the cool weather comes. For best results plant basil seeds indoors in mid-April and then transplant the plants outside in early June or when the weather turns warm.

Vegetables can be divided into categories of cool weather (peas, spinach and lettuce) and warm weather (beans, peppers and tomatoes). Warm weather vegetables are best sown indoors and then transplanted outdoors or purchased as a bedding plant from a nursery and set out sometime between May 24 and June 1.

For most transplants it is wise to replant them at the same depth as they were grown. One exception is tomato plants that should always be planted two fingers deeper so they will develop additional roots on the stalk. Be sure to leave room in the pot for expansion or additional growth unless they are growing up or over the edge of the pot.

Tomatoes need to be staked or contained with hoops. Beans and cucumbers can be supported by several bamboo stakes tied in tepee fashion but they grow best on netting that will also serve as a green screen.

As plants begin to grow, they will need to be fertilized regularly. Apply 20.20.20 or 15.30.15 fertilizer at half strength every week depending on whether you want more leaf growth or flower and seed growth. Add new plants as you harvest the mature ones.

Choosing your plants may be easier if you have themes for your containers. Here are a few suggestions:
- Salsa Garden: Tomato, pepper, cilantro and onion
- Pesto Pot: Basil, garlic and parsley
- Rainbow Planter: Tomato, eggplant, peppers (all colours) and purple basil
- Stir-fry Collection: Chinese eggplant, hot pepper, snow pea and bok choy
- Salad Bowl: Mesculin mix, tomato, pepper, radish and cucumber,
- Pizza Sauce: Tomato, green pepper, onions and oregano,

- Kid's Korner: Radish, tomato, bush bean, basil and carrots as a follow up crop to early maturing radish.

Check out your balcony, patio, sundeck or window boxes and see if you have room for a food crop this summer.

Converting a Lawn to a Vegetable Garden

Should you decide to convert a section of lawn into a vegetable garden do not haul the turf away. Cut the turf into rectangular blocks of manageable size and stack the moist blocks upside down in a meter square area in the middle of your new garden. Between each layer of turf add a light dusting of lawn or high nitrogen fertilizer. Cover the pile of inverted lawn sod with black plastic and tie a cord around the base to secure the plastic. After six to eight months or the next growing season you can cut small holes in the plastic on the sides or top of the pile and plant seed potatoes that will grow and cascade down the sides of the pile. Any heat-loving plant such as corn, cucumbers, squash or pumpkin will also respond well in a pile of old turf. At the end of the season remove the plastic and spread the well-decayed turf over the rest of your vegetable garden. If you have access to waste turf, the procedure can be repeated until you have enough top soil for your raised beds.

Vegetable Growing Chart

Vegetable	Soil Temp. for Germ. (°C)	Fertilizer	pH	Main Problems
Asparagus	20 – 25	4.10.10	6–7	Aphids & dry soil
Beans	16 – 29	6.15. 9	6–7.5	Aphids & slugs
Broad Beans	5 – 15	4.10.10	5.5–6.5	Aphids & flea beetles
Beets	10 – 29	5.15.10	5.8–7	Leaf miners

Vegetable	Soil Temp. for Germ. (°C)	Fertilizer	pH	Main Problems
Broccoli	10 – 20	4.10.10 + 34 N at new growth	6 – 7	Cabbage maggot, clubroot
Brussels Sprouts	See broccoli & cabbage			Black leg & black rot
Cabbage	7 – 20	4.10.10 + extra N	5.5 – 7	Same as broccoli
Carrot	15 – 20	6.15.10	5.5 – 7	Carrot fly, dry soil, rocks
Cauliflower	15	4.10.10	6 – 7	See broccoli & cabbage
Celery	18	4.10.10 + N	6 – 6.5	Carrot fly & dry soil
Corn	21 – 35	4.15.10 + 7 extra N at mid term	6 – 7	Corn borers & raccoons
Cucumber	21 – 35	6 K before 6.12.6 + 4 N at vine stage	6 – 8	Vine worms, slugs.
Dill	15 – 20	10.13.13	5.5 – 7	Aphids & green worms
Eggplant	18 – 27	5. 6. 4	6 – 7	Aphids & flee beetles
Leeks	10 – 15	4.10.10 + N	6 – 8	Onion maggots
Lettuce	4 – 20	10.12.6	6 – 7	Slugs, leaf rot
Onions	9 – 32	6.15.16	6.5 – 7	Onion maggots
Parsnip	5 – 20	6.15.12	6 – 8	Carrot fly and shallow soil
Parsley	15 – 20	4.10.10	5 – 7	Carrot fly
Peas	4 – 14	0. 9. 6	6 – 7	Powdery mildew, weevils
Peppers	16 – 24	5. 6. 4	6 – 7	Aphids, cutworms, flea beetles
Potatoes	5 – 20	4.10.10	4.8 – 5.6	Scab, flea beetle
Pumpkin				See cucumber
Radish	5 – 15	6.15.15	6 – 8	Maggots, dry soil
Rhubarb		4.10.10	5 – 6.8	Divide every 7 to 10 years

Vegetable	Soil Temp. for Germ. (°C)	Fertilizer	pH	Main Problems
Spinach	4 -15	15.15.15	6.2 – 6.9	Bolts with long days
Squash	See cucumber			
Swiss Chard	10 – 29	5.15.10	5.8 – 7	Leaf miners, dry soil
Tomatoes	24 +	8.10.6 Plus 2 N as fruit starts	6 – 7	Flee beetles, blossom end rot
Turnip	15	4.10.10	6 – 8	Maggots and clubroot

* Fertilizer values are given as a guide and are not based on commonly produced commercial fertilizers. Choose a fertilizer that has similar proportions.

CHAPTER FIFTEEN

Annuals & Perennials

Gardening terminology can be a problem when dealing with the topic of annuals and perennials. A definition of terms may help reduce the confusion about how these plants are categorized.

- **Annual**: Any herbaceous type plant that grows, flowers, sets seed and dies in the course of one year.

- **Perennial**: Any herbaceous type plant that has the ability to alternate between growing and lying dormant for a period of three or more years. Most perennials bloom the second year after seeding and each year thereafter.

- **Biennial**: Any herbaceous plant that grows one year, flowers and sets seed in the second or third year and then dies. These plants are often referred to as short-lived perennials.

The division between a large woody perennial and a soft low growing shrub is sometimes difficult to determine. Another division is the categorization of bulbs. They are perennials but are usually treated as a sub group.

Another confusing factor is climate. Tender geraniums growing in the Pacific Northwest are classed as annuals because they die when hit with the first hard frost. In frost free areas such as Mexico they continue to grow and are classed as perennials. Add to this the fact that there are tender and hardy varieties of the same plant. Tender geraniums and fuchsia will not tolerate frost whereas the hardy varieties of these plants will.

Annuals are generally quick to mature and bloom after seeding. They most often provide continuous bloom until they die in the Fall. Perennials generally do not bloom until the second year after seeding and the blooming period is often limited to three to six weeks. For long term seasonal colour, perennial beds need a succession of blooms using a variety of plants.

Comparing Annuals to Perennials *(Some Generalizations)*

Annuals	Perennials
5 to 6 months of bloom	3 to 6 weeks of bloom
higher cost	lower cost
shorter term	longer term
short and compact	taller and less compact
replant annually	replant every 3 to 5 years
soil is improved each year	soil is mulched every year or two
more cultivation, fewer weeds	less cultivation, more weeds and grass
requires more watering	requires less watering
bare bed in the winter	green or brown bed in the winter
inter planted with spring bulbs	bulbs are naturalized in bed

Plant Choice and Design

All gardeners have their own idea as to what an annual or perennial bed should look like. Some people prefer to mix their annuals, perennials, bulbs and shrubs together while others may choose to concentrate various plants in select beds. Whether you prefer something on the wild or natural side, or a more formal style, is a personal choice.

The shape and style of the bed will have a large impact on the appearance of the garden. Curved and raised beds are much less formal than rectangular flat beds.

Both flower and foliage colour can change the overall look of the garden. Cool colours such as blues, purples and white create a different feeling than warm colours such as reds, oranges, yellows and browns. Using white and light grey as contrasting colours will make pinks, reds, blues and purples look more intense. Using a monochromatic or one colour theme can also be very effective. This works well with a range of blues and purples, pinks or yellows and oranges. The opposite to monochromatic is polychromatic where all colours are used and no dominant colours clash. There can also be a wide range of leaf colours ranging from light yellow-green to dark grey-green. Grey, purple and variegated will also be part of the palette.

Flower and leaf shape and size can add character to a garden. A few large canna lilies with bold blooms will create quite a different look than a mound of cushion mums with button size flowers. The more large leafed plants in a garden the more lush and tropical it will look. Yellow or yellow-green variegated leaves in low light or shaded areas will reflect more light and brighten that section of a garden.

Buying Annuals and Perennials

The natural tendency when buying plants is to go for the larger more expensive ones. Remember smaller pots and younger plants are easier to transplant and you can buy several small ones for the price of one big one. Perennials in # 1 pots are plants that may have outgrown their small pots and have been recently

Feature entrance bed.

transplanted. You may not be getting that much more for your money. Check the root structure and make sure both annual and perennial plants are not pot bound. Look in the pot drain holes for slugs and other hitchhikers that you do not want in your garden. Insects and insect eggs can be hidden under the leaves of plants that have been sitting around the nursery for long periods.

Using a sheet or two of graph paper draw a simple plan of the bed to be planted. A planting plan will help determine the choice of plants, their location in the bed, how many plants you will need and the cost. If the cost is too high you may have to scale back the plan. Buying too many or too few plants means a second trip to the nursery.

Positioning of Plants

There is more to planting than putting the root ball in the soil. Height will determine if the plant should go in the foreground, middle ground or background. Stacking plants by height will create the effect of tilting the bed which will display more colour to the viewer.

Not all plants need full sun and some will be unhappy if placed in a hot, dry location. The reverse is true for those sun lovers that end up in deep shade.

The role of basic colour is often overlooked when planting. Light colours at the front of a bed and darker colours at the back tend to give the illusion of depth the same as in a painting. Sharp colours will lead the eye and distract from areas that are less attractive. The use of white and grey help to provide contrast and make darker colours appear to be more intense. White flowers in the garden will come into prominence before sunrise and after sunset creating the appearance of illumination.

Planting Annuals

Many annual beds double as spring bulb beds and the bulb leaves and/or the bulbs have to be removed before the bed is prepared for summer annuals. Add 2.5 to 5 cm of compost or aged manure to the bed and till it in. In high rainfall areas where the pH is always being pulled down it will be necessary to add dolomite lime at the rate of about 2 kg /10m^2. Supplementary fertilizer can also be added at this time at a rate recommended by the manufacturer rake or cultivate in the lime and fertilizer before planting.

The mature size of each annual will determine the spacing of plants. When plants are mature there should be no bare soil showing in the bed. This not only gives a fuller look but prevents weeds from gaining a foothold.

Young annuals that come in pots with two or more plants need to be teased apart with as little damage to the roots as possible. Slip your fingers between the stems and turn the pot upside down to shake the plants out. Dig a hole large enough to allow the roots to be spread out if possible. If fertilizer was not added to the bed during the initial preparation a tablespoon of fertilizer can be added to the hole and thoroughly mixed with the soil before planting. Make sure the new plant is at the same level that it was in the pot and pack the soil around the root ball. Water the plants as soon as they have been planted to help reduce shock and to drive out excess air. Using boards or a strip of plywood in the bed to walk on reduces soil compaction.

Planting Perennials

Annuals are always planted in the spring but there is a range of times for planting perennials. Traditionally, perennials were sold in nurseries as year old plants in the spring. This may not be the best time as the soil in the early spring is very cold and by the late spring when the soil is warmer the plants have not had time to develop a good root structure before they are programmed to bloom. Planting in the fall takes advantage of the warm soil and cool weather, which reduces the shock of transplanting. Roots have an opportunity to start their growth and be ready for an early start in the spring. Potted perennials can also be planted in the summer but will require more care, especially regular watering.

The location and method of planting a perennial will depend on the plant and its particular environmental needs. Most perennials prefer full sun and can be planted in a traditional perennial border bed. Other plants may be adapted to shade and planted in a woodland garden under a canopy of trees. Alpine or rock garden specimens will need very well drained soil and full sun.

When planting a new perennial bed it is advisable to work in a generous quantity of compost or aged manure to the soil after all the roots and rocks have been removed. This can be done by digging or roto-tilling. As with annuals most west coast soils will need an application of dolomite lime at 2 kg / 10m². The potted plants can then be set out and properly spaced before actually digging any holes. Knock the root balls out of the pots and examine the roots to see if they are pot bound. Trim off some of the older and darker non-feeding roots and try to gently pull the root ball apart and spread the roots if possible. As a general rule the root mass should be planted slightly above the soil level to allow for compaction. In newly-tilled beds soil can settle over time. Start planting at the back and work to the front of the bed. Adding a layer of mulch to a new perennial bed will help conserve moisture and feed the microbes that are so essential to the health of the plants and the soil. Worms will convert and transport much of the organic matter down into the root zone. Once the bed is fully planted it should be watered thoroughly to remove any air pockets (they prevent capillary action) and provide moisture for the new plants.

When adding plants to existing beds the root ball can be planted in the existing soil and then mulched and watered. Planting perennials in a woodland garden can be more difficult because of the mass of existing roots The smaller the plant the easier it is to find a place to dig a hole between the roots. Add some compost mulch and water regularly if the soil is dry.

Experienced gardeners prepare raised beds augmented with grit and sand to improve drainage before planting any alpine or rock garden plants. Do not use a mulch on an alpine type planting.

Soil that has been improved with compost or manure and mulched with more compost will not need any additional fertilizer. However, some heavy feeders such as roses, lilies and delphiniums will benefit from more fertilizer.

Wide perennial beds are sometimes difficult to access without causing compaction. Installing a few well placed flat stepping stones or old fence boards behind the plants will allow access without the compaction. The boards will also serve as slug traps because each time you enter the bed you can turn over the board and kill the resident slugs.

Preparing the Annual Flower Bed

Each spring gardeners attempt to create flowerbeds that will be bulging with growth and radiant with colour. By August the results may not be up to expectations because basic concepts have not been fully understood. Gardeners might find this checklist helpful before starting their planting and spring garden routine.

Is the flower bed in the right location as part of the overall landscape plan? Sometimes by making a small change in the layout, the flower bed will be more visible or better integrated into the rest of the garden design.

Developing a proper setting for a flower bed can also be important. Is there a nice backdrop, lawn or series of shrubs to make the bed look natural?

Beds that are long and narrow, square or perfect circles are generally not as attractive as those with gentle curved lines and irregular shapes.

Choosing plants for the bed is the most critical decision of all because several factors have to be considered. If the area is shaded or partially shaded the list of plants to choose from is greatly reduced. A sun loving plant grown in the shade will not perform up to its potential.

Plant height is often overlooked when planning but can be a most significant factor. To achieve the best results plants should be planted with low ones in the front and tall ones in the back. A sloping or near vertical wall of colour is usually more dramatic than a flat uniform flower bed. Sometimes the height required to give a flower bed interest can be achieved by using a feature plant in the center of the bed and then arranging the other shorter plants around the feature plant. This technique also allows for a distinct change in leaf shape or flower colour.

Colour choices are an individual decision but there are a number of well accepted rules to follow. You can go with a single colour or use two colours for contrast. When using more than one colour make sure they complement one another. ie. red and green, blue and orange, or yellow and purple. A second way to use a variation of colour is to choose one colour and then use lighter or darker shades of that same colour. Pink is the most common monochromatic choice going from almost white to near red. Orange can vary from near yellow to brown while purple can vary from white to deep blue. Achieving contrast using white petals or silver grey foliage is often overlooked or not fully appreciated by gardeners. The white or grey will make most other colours look more intense and give the garden bed a vibrancy in the early morning and late evening when the light is less intense. Too many different colours or a random mixture might give the bed a cluttered look.

No matter how good your artistic plans are, the ultimate look of the bed will depend on the growth of the plants. To achieve healthy growth and good colour, the soil in the beds must be prepared and enriched to provide continuous feeding during the entire growing season. Remove the dead leaves from your spring flowering bulbs and dig or cultivate the bed taking care not to disturb the bulbs. Add a two to three inch layer of compost or

Ornamental pool and flower garden.

well rotted manure to the bed plus a good application of lime (particularly for high rainfall areas). Dig the compost or manure into the bed so it is mixed with the soil but not more then two to four inches deep. The organic material must stay in the root zone. Lay a scrap of plywood or board in the bed to stand on and start planting from the back. Use your trowel to measure the spacing and dig a small hole for each bedding plant. If the soil is poor each plant will benefit from an ounce or two of 4-10-10 fertilizer mixed with the soil in the hole before planting. Firm the plant to ensure that the root ball will be able to draw moisture from the surrounding soil and then water to give the plant a good start. As the plants grow the spaces between them will disappear and there will be no room for weeds. Plants that are growing in rich soil with sufficient water and adequate sunlight are less likely to be bothered by pests. I hope you will incorporate these basic ideas into your spring garden plans and enjoy the results all summer.

CHAPTER 16

Ferns & Mosses

Most gardeners in the Pacific Northwest spend a great deal of time scraping moss out of garden beds and combing it out of lawns. Moss loves shade and moisture and the Pacific Northwest certainly has the ideal growing conditions.

Instead of constantly fighting the growth of moss, it might make more sense to use moss as a ground cover and landscape feature. This will reduce your costs and time spent on garden maintenance.

Moss is an important aspect in Japanese gardens. It is widely used around water features where there is misting or high humidity. The character of large rocks or boulders along streams can be changed by allowing moss to grow on them. The edge or capping on pools can be softened with the addition of moss colonies. Rock gardens or difficult shady slopes can be stabilized using large blankets of moss. Some perennial beds and woodland gardens look best with an understory or carpet of moss. Pathways covered in moss will tolerate low traffic.

Lawn areas that are in almost constant shade are much better converted to a moss groundcover. Converting all or part of your lawn to moss will reduce the amount of mowing and watering required. In the spring you can cut back on the amount of moss killer, lime and fertilizer you would normally apply. De-thatching of moss areas will no longer be necessary. With few, if any, weeds and no diseases or pests to worry about there will be no need for herbicides and pesticides. A moss ground cover, however, will not stand up to heavy use by children or dogs.

Mosses are very primitive plants that reproduce vegetatively or by spores. They do not have true roots and all their nutrients come from the air or rain. Moss does not compete directly with other plants, except for space. Most mosses have the ability to spread very quickly when introduced into an ideal location. They are extremely hardy and can withstand both high and low temperatures. Under adverse conditions mosses can go dormant for months and then spring back to life when the weather warms or it begins to rain.

Establishing a Moss Garden

To establish a moss garden, the area should be raked free of all leaves and organic debris. The base should be a firmly packed mineral soil that is low in nutrients and has a pH between 5 and 6. Dappled or full shade will ensure long periods of high humidity during summer irrigation or winter rain, a set of conditions that is typical of many Northwest gardens.

Once the moss is established, it requires very little care. Weeding may be necessary while the moss is colonizing the area, but most common weeds prefer more sun and nutrients. Regular watering is important when the moss is first planted.

There are some 700 species of native mosses on the Pacific Northwest coast, no doubt a reflection of the wet marine climate. Interesting moss colonies for introduction into your garden can be found on roadsides, under power lines or on construction sites. Do not remove moss for transplanting from parks, greenbelts or sensitive ecological areas.

Native mosses vary greatly in colour, displaying a wide range of greens along with hints of copper, red and yellow. Look for some of the club mosses or other species that grow much higher than common lawn moss to give variation in height. Moss will also look great as feature colonies in the rock garden.

Rather than fight the presence of moss in your garden, it might be better to embrace it and reduce your labour and costs.

The Hardy Fern

Some gardeners tend to dismiss ferns as uninteresting garden plants because they do not produce flowers. In spite of their lack of colour, they give a garden aesthetic qualities that are difficult to achieve using other plants. They add a soft, graceful appearance and can act as a neutral backdrop or foil for other flowering and accent plants. Their ability to grow in sun or shade with low nutrient demands makes them ideal for those difficult spots.

Many of the larger ferns, when grown in numbers, can give a garden a tropical appearance or a primeval look. I recall walking through a fern forest and water garden in New Zealand and thinking how lush and exotic it was.

Ferns, or pteridophytes as they are called, make up a huge group of plants—some 12,000 species in all. Most (about 80%) grow in the humid tropics, an area often associated with ferns. Surprisingly, some (5%) are found in dry or desert areas. The balance grow in cool damp woodland areas, and the Pacific Northwest climate is ideal for most of these varieties, including native species.

Until 1991, all ferns grown in this area were herbaceous, meaning they have no woody stem or trunk and are low. Then the first major attempt to import and grow the Tasmanian tree fern (*Dicksonia antarctica*) was undertaken by a local nursery. So far the survival rate looks promising and the availability of these unique landscaping plants will no doubt increase.

Planting Ferns

If you would like to add some tropical character to your garden, the best time to plant ferns is in the late fall or early spring when the plants are dormant. Dig a hole one and a half times the depth of the root ball, or of the pot in which the fern is growing. Before planting, mix two measures of loose soil with one measure of coarse compost. A little bone meal mixed into the soil will provide slow release phosphorous to assist in root development. Keep the new plant at the same depth as it was growing before replanting.

Most Pacific Northwest ferns grow in a forested setting where a natural leaf mould will develop above the root structure. Try to approximate this leaf mould with a layer of compost or mulch. This will help keep the fern cool and moist, and provide a slow but steady source of nutrients.

There are a half dozen ferns that are native to our area and all but one is useful in the garden. Lady (*Athyrium felix-femina*), Deer (*Blechnum spicant*), Sword (*Polystichum munitum*), Maidenhair (*Asplenium trichomanes*) and Licorice (*Polypodium glycyrrhiza*) ferns are all good garden plants when used in the right place. The only weed in the group is the Bracken or Brake fern (*Pteridium aquilinum*) which grows on a tall central stock up to six feet high and should not be added to your garden.

Propagate Your Fern

It is possible to propagate ferns in several ways, but check first to see which growth pattern the fern has. Some ferns form multiple crowns, which can be divided and replanted. Others form rhizomes or rhizomatous roots and sections of the root can be severed and dug to form new plants. A small group of ferns form buds or offsets that may be separated and replanted.

Propagation by Spores. Propagation by spores will produce new plants but it will require a year or more. Fill a shallow, wide mouth glass jar half full with moist mica-peat and sprinkle the spores on the surface. Cover the container with plastic wrap and seal with an elastic band. Place the container in indirect light and keep the temperature between 15° and 18°C until the spores develop a prothalus. This will look like a tiny flat green leaf lying on the surface of the peat. As the prothalus develops, the male and female parts of the spore come together and form a tiny new fern. When the sporlings are large enough, pick them out of the mica-peat and pot them up. Transplant them out in the garden when they are 8 to 10 cm (3″ to 4″) high.

Fern Maintenance

The only annual maintenance that hardy ferns require is the removal of the fronds in the spring. All the old fronds should be cut off in March just before the new shoots (fiddle heads) emerge. The old fronds can be ground into a mulch with a power mower and placed at the base of the fern or added to the compost for next year's compost mulch. Whole fronds will not break down in the compost.

Yuccas and deer ferns after pruning.

Amending Soil with Peat Moss

Peat moss is a common soil amendment, and an organic supplement, but how valuable is it? Before answering, we need to know something about the character and source of peat moss.

Actually, there are two forms of peat that are used in gardening. One is sedge peat which is found in lowland bog areas that

Fern fronds converted to mulch with lawn mower.

are poorly drained. Most sedge peat is the remains of sedges, rushes and marsh-like plants that are partially decomposed. The rate of decomposition under these conditions is generally very slow due to the acidic nature of the bog or wetland. Although there are exceptions to the rule, it is difficult to find a peat that is not acidic. As more peat is formed on the top, the bottom layers become compacted and over a very long time will turn into soft brown coal.

For centuries the Irish have been cutting peat, or "turf" as they call it, to burn as fuel in their homes and in thermal generating plants. The deeper, more compact layers of peat contain wax and, when dried, make a better fuel. Here in the Pacific Northwest, large areas of weathered sedge peat can be cultivated and planted but may require drainage and liming. This type of soil is referred to as muckland and can be found along rivers and wetlands.

The other type of peat is sphagnum and it is the partially decayed strands of sphagnum moss, a plant that will grow in shallow water around the edges of bogs, marshes and small lakes. With a high rainfall, the moss can raise itself above the water table after it totally chokes the water body. As new moss grows, it pushes old moss down under the acidic water where very little decay will occur. In old, well-established sphagnum peat bogs, the pH can be as low as 3. At this level of acidity, along with low oxygen levels, few bacteria survive to cause decay.

In recent years there has been some concern about the destruction of peat bogs for the commercial production of peat moss. Sphagnum peat tends to grow quickly under the right conditions, and is a renewable resource. If the harvesting rate and growth rate are balanced, the supply should last forever. My son introduced some live sphagnum moss into our fish pool and now I have to harvest a pail full every year to keep it under control. However, sedge peat does not regenerate itself as readily.

Both types of peat are used as soil conditioners but sphagnum is usually reserved for the higher quality potting soils, and the sedge peats are used in the large volume, lower value topsoils. Their most important characteristic is the ability to add water-holding qualities to the soil. Sedge peat will hold between 5 and 7 times its weight in water and sphagnum twice that much! This may be a disadvantage in our high rainfall area where drainage is poor.

Peat will also break up compacted soils that have a high clay content. With more air holes and lightweight material between the soil particles, peat lightens the soil and makes it easier for roots to grow.

Sphagnum peat has been reported to have anti-fungal properties that are certainly useful when preparing soil-less mixes for starting seeds. However, coming from an acidic bog, spagnum peat is not rich in microbial life, which must be present for good growth beyond the seedling stage. The addition of a small amount of soil will help when peat is used in such things as commercially sold "grow bags". The nutritional or fertilizer value of peat is very low and combined with a low pH, the nutrients that are there may not be available to the plants without the addition of lime.

A 3-cubic-foot bale of sphagnum peat costs two or three times as much as bagged commercial compost or steer manure. The compost and manure both have far more nutrients and microbial activity. Home compost is similar and, apart from the labour, is free.

While peat moss has some beneficial characteristics and uses, to increase the volume, water-holding capacity and nutrient level of your soil, it is hard to beat manure or compost.

CHAPTER SEVENTEEN

Groundcovers & Rockery Plants

Lawns are by far the most common groundcovers, creating a very soft and pleasing setting for suburban homes. The use of grass as a groundcover is not without its problems, particularly if you want a high-quality turf. With liming, de-thatching, de-mossing, aerating and fertilizing in the spring and then regular weeding, watering and mowing for the remainder of the growing season, many hours of work and considerable expense is required. What are the alternatives?

Groundcovers other than lawns might be a sensible choice if you are tired of mowing grass that serves little purpose other than creating a pleasant visual effect.

Before considering the use of groundcovers you should be aware of their advantages and disadvantages. By their very nature groundcovers are grown to quickly cover an area and sometimes they spread so rapidly that they become invasive. If they are difficult to control or eradicate, they may create more work, not less. In some cases the plant material can be prickly and hard to prune or clean up.

Plants used for ground cover may be ideal in some locations but create problems in others. For example, in the fall a large maple tree may drop a heavy layer of leaves on the groundcover, making it difficult to rake. Small birch leaves, on the other hand, falling down into a similar groundcover will be fine as they will form a mulch at ground level where they cannot be seen.

A good groundcover should provide total coverage in a specific area in order to help suppress weed growth. Plants used for groundcover should be relatively inexpensive because of the numbers that are required. They should also be easy to maintain and evergreen or at least have some branch colour to be beneficial during the winter.

When planting groundcovers as a lawn replacement, a common mistake is to use a single variety that is relatively low in height. In most cases it is far better to incorporate several varieties into your landscape plan so you can have a variety of heights, colours and leaf types. Using the right combination of groundcovers will enable you to create a multi-level effect that will add interest to a garden setting. Different heights of groundcovers can create the illusion of a rolling or tiered area and disguise a relatively flat landscape.

Before choosing a groundcover, make sure you know the specific growing conditions of the area. Various plant species respond to very different environmental requirements. To get the best and quickest results, match the groundcover to the area's conditions: sun or shade, moisture or dryness, acid or alkaline, etc.

There are dozens of choices of groundcover plants. Here are a few you might like to consider:

Low Varieties: 5 to 10 cm (2 to 4 in)
Ajuga reptans, *Cornus canadensis*, Moss varieties, *Phlox subulata*, *Rubus pentalobus*, Sedum varieties, *Sempervivum tectorum* and Thyme varieties. Of this group the *Ajuga* will grow in the sun but is better suited to light or deep shade. *Rubus* may not be hardy at higher elevations or during very cold winters. *Sempervivum* is best on dry sunny banks.

Semi-Low Varieties: 10 to 30 cm (4 to 12 in)
Anagallis monelli, *Arctostaphylos uva ursi*, Erica varieties, Calluna

varieties, *Euonymus fortunei, Galtheria procumbens*, Hedera varieties, *Hypericum calycinum, Iberis sempervirens,* Juniper varieties, *Pachysandra terminalis, Stachys lanata, Tolmiea menziesi,* Vaccinium varieties and Vinca minor varieties. The shade lovers here are *Galtheria, Hedera, Pachysandra, Tolmiea Vaccinium* and *Vinca minor,* although they will grow in partial sun. *Hypericum* is very invasive and should only be used where it is bordered by concrete. *Tolmiea* is native to our cool, damp streambeds and can also be used as a house plant (Piggyback plant).

Medium Varieties: 10 to 60 cm (4 to 24 in)
Blechnum spicant, Calluna varieties, *Cotoneaster dammeri* or *macrophyllus,* Erica varieties, *Genista pilosa,* Hemerocallis varieties and Hosta varieties. *Hemerocallis* and *Hosta* are not evergreen and will not stand by themselves as a year-round groundcover. Cotoneaster is prone to being too rampant unless it is pruned frequently. *Calluna* and *Erica* need full sun.

High Varieties: 90 cm plus (36 in and higher)
Cornus varieties, Cytisus varieties, *Polystichum munitum, Athyrim filix femina,* Laurel varieties (Otto Luyken and Zabeliana), Mahonia varieties, Potentilla varieties and Rosa varieties (shrub). *Cornus* is not evergreen but some varieties come with red or yellow bark and are very attractive in the winter sunshine. *Mahonia* and ferns will do quite well in partial sun or shade.

No matter which ground cover you use, there will always be a moderate amount of maintenance involved. When the plants are first established, it is essential to keep the area weed free until the entire ground area is covered. In later years you will spend less time weeding and more time pruning and trimming to prevent the more rampant growers from overrunning other plants or walkways.

To reduce watering, deter weeds, save labour and provide more nutrients for the plants, do not remove the dead leaves from under the higher groundcovers or shrubs. Sweep the leaves that land on the beds or walks in under the canopy of branches.

Plants for the Rockery and Rock Wall

For many years I visited Victoria each March and was always impressed by the show of spring colour, especially in the many rock gardens throughout the city. With a lower rainfall and numerous rocky outcrops, Victoria and the Capital Regional District are well suited to this style of garden.

More moist areas in the Pacific Northwest may not have such ideal growing conditions for rockery plants but they can flourish under less than ideal conditions and put on a great show each spring.

There is no standard definition for rockery type plants and anything that will grow in a traditional rock garden or wall area can be included in the group. Many are alpine in origin and grow less than 15cm (6") high but these may spread to several feet in diameter.

Rockery plants provide great spring colour and soften the appearance of rock walls.

Planting and Maintaining Rockery Plants

The best conditions for rockery plants are southern exposure, well-drained soil and a surface of large rocks, stone walls or other hard materials on which to grow.

Concrete retaining walls are often excellent sites for rockery plants. When used in this location, try to train the plants to grow down and cover between 1/3 and 2/3 of the wall for the best effect. Also, vary the length of the plants that hang over the wall to create a more natural look. Plants should be placed as close to the front of the wall as possible. Small hardy type bulbs can be planted to grow up between the clumps of plants or come up through them.

With lock blocks, rubble or dry walls, plants can be placed between the stones at the time of building or inserted afterwards. The appearance of an uneven or weathered wall can be spruced up and softened with the addition of flowering plants.

One lovely old courtyard in England I visited was paved in patio stones about a metre square. All the 5 cm (2") gaps between the stones were planted with an array of rockery plants. Each one was a different height with a different leaf and foliage colour. The mounds of colour and greenery spilling on to the patio stones created an excellent effect.

Seeds are available but most will require some specialized care to germinate and grow to transplanting size.

The ideal time to purchase new plants is when you see them blooming in local gardens. Try one or two plants of several varieties and plant them where you want more colour. Within a year you should know which ones are well suited to your particular conditions.

The majority of rockery plants stay green most of the year and have a diverse blooming schedule. By choosing the right plants, your rock garden or rock wall can have colour from March through August with almost every colour in the spectrum being displayed.

The maintenance of a rock garden can be a problem if the area is badly infested with weeds. Regular weeding is essential but the care of the plants themselves is quite easy. Most are drought tolerant. A light application of compost each year with some supplementary "low nitrogen" fertilizer (i.e., 4.10.10) will keep your plants growing and flowering. Wood ashes are a good source of potash (potassium) and will help to raise the pH level.

If your plants suffer from partial winterkill or look straggly in the spring, prune them back to some live buds and force them to bush out again. In wet climates some plants will be over-run with moss. Spray with moss killer (iron sulphate) and comb out the moss to allow the plants more light, heat and dryness.

Many gardeners assume rock garden perennials will only bloom once per year. To encourage the plant to put out a second or even a third flush of flowers, you should deadhead the old flower stalks as soon as they begin to deteriorate.

When the plants become well established it is easy to propagate many of the plants by division. If you don't want to risk cutting into them, try layering the longer stems and see if they will form roots some distance from the crown of the plant.

Those who have a keen interest in rockery type plants may wish to join a local alpine plant club and take advantage of their plant sales and seed exchange as well as the expert knowledge they have to share.

CHAPTER EIGHTEEN

Vines & Trellises

Clematis

Clematis is one of the easiest and most rewarding vines you can grow. It is relatively free of diseases and can provide a lifetime of enjoyment. The showy blooms range in size from 2½ cm (1") to the size of a luncheon plate, with a full range of colours from which to choose.

Clematis are indigenous to the temperate world, with species coming from Asia, Europe, North America and New Zealand. English gardeners first began cultivation of the clematis at the time of Elizabeth I, and from this early introduction came most of the early hybrid varieties. Today, hybridizers from half a dozen countries are producing some magnificent varieties. One local grower in the Fraser Valley propagates well over a hundred varieties and this wide selection of plants has created a problem for home gardeners. How does one make the right choice and then care for the plant once it is in your garden?

Vines that are found in the wild are called *species clematis*. They generally bloom in early to mid spring and the flowers form on mature wood or wood that was formed the previous summer. The flowers are usually small but come in a wide range of colours. Because flowers form on mature wood, the vines should not be pruned hard but trimmed lightly, if necessary, after flowering. Some well known species clematis are: *alpina, macropetala, montana, texensis* and *viticella.*

One unique type of species clematis is *Armandi.* It is the only

Clematis montana 'Rubens': Type A, no pruning required.

evergreen variety and therefore has a special role to play in land-scaping. Unlike most deciduous clematis, it is on the tender side and will often be damaged by frost, particularly at higher elevations, and is best grown up against the house or in a sheltered location. No regular pruning is required.

The opposite of species clematis are hybrids and they generally fall into three categories. One group will bloom in late May or June, and the other two in July and again possibly in September. The hybrids generally have large flowers in a wide range of colours, including variegations.

Pruning Clematis

Most of the late spring bloomers form their flowers on semi-ripened wood and don't require regular pruning. The grower's tag will often say "pruning optional" which means they will still produce flowers if pruned, but the blooms will be much later. They are such rampant growers that cutting them to the ground every three or four years helps to keep them looking more attractive.

Nellie Moser clematis: Type B1, pruning optional.

Some examples are: Mrs. Cholmondeley, W.E. Gladstone, Barbara Dibley and Crimson King.

Summer blooming clematis produce flowers on both new growth and old growth and there is no easy way to know which is which. Check the grower's tag, if available. For those plants that flower on new growth, it is recommended that you cut them down to 30 to 50 cm (18") each year. Cut just above a leaf node as this is where the dormant bud is, and that will produce next year's growth. Cutting the vine at this point will also cause several more stems to shoot from the base of the plant. In areas where you want the flowers to be particularly high on a trellis or railing, it might be best to cut the old vine at 2 or 3 metres instead of 50 cm.

Most books recommend cutting back these clematis in the spring but I think it is better to do it in early December after the first heavy frost. This way you do not have to look at the brown vines all winter.

Some examples of the "Prune Hard" variety are: Gypsy Queen, Jackmanii, Perle d'Azur, Comtesse de Bouchard, Ernest Markham, Ville de Lyon and John Huxtable. Examples of "No Pruning Required" are: The President, Blue Ravine , Ramona, Vyvyan Pennell, Duchess of Edinburgh, Henryi and Nellie Moser. These plants, like the "Pruning Optional" above, are best cut back every few years to keep them tidy and under control.

Just remember that all clematis will tolerate pruning. The only difference is that some of them take a while to develop enough semi-ripe or mature wood to set flowers. If you make a mistake, you may just have to wait a few months or a year to see blooms.

Growing Clematis

Most *species clematis*, in their native habitat grow on the edge of a forest clearing. Wind or birds carry the seeds to trees where they are dropped in the damp mulch below the branches. After they

Clematis Chart

Group	Evergreen or Deciduous?	Species or Hybrid ?	Bloom Time	Bloom Colour	Bloom Size	Blooms On?	Pruning	Example	Note
A	Deciduous	Species	May	Range	2-3"	Mature wood	None required	C. Montana	Trim after flowering. Remove dead wood. Very rampant.
	Evergreen	Species	March	White	2-3"	Mature wood	None required	C. Armandi	Not very cold hardy.
B1	Deciduous	Hybrid	May-June Sept?	Range	4-8"	Mature wood or new mature	Every 2-4 years	Nellie Moser	Prune in February.
B2									
C	Deciduous	Hybrid	June to Sept	Range	4-8"	Mature wood or new wood	2-4 yrs or every year B1 or C	The President	Prune in December.

germinate in this cool, damp environment, they climb up through the lower branches seeking light and pop their heads out into the sun. The flowers form on the cascading vines where they have full sun. If a tree is not available, a clematis will happily scramble over large stumps, dead trees, rock outcroppings or fences.

Knowing these basic growing habits of clematis helps determine where to plant the vine to achieve the best results. The rule of thumb is, "Keep their feet in the shade and their heads in the sun." Vines will always grow towards the sun.

When planting a clematis on a fence, always plant assuming that the vine will want to grow southward for two to four metres. Some training may be required to encourage the vine to follow the fence in an east or west direction. If the fence runs east-west

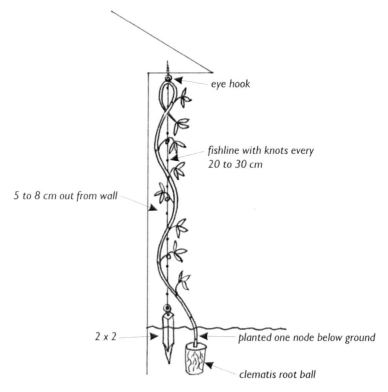

eye hook

fishline with knots every 20 to 30 cm

5 to 8 cm out from wall

2 x 2

planted one node below ground

clematis root ball

Clematis support on house wall

and you live on the north side, the clematis will not produce many flowers on your side but will benefit your neighbours. The same is true when planting vines on arbors or pergolas.

A clematis vine is planted permanently and should be given a rich soil to grow in. Dig a hole 30 to 45 cm in diameter and in depth, and mix two-thirds of the excavated soil with one-third compost or well rotted manure. A handful of bonemeal and a handful of lime will provide extra phosphorous and raise the pH of the soil. Place the clematis root ball in the hole so the first leaf node on the vine is 2-3 cm below the soil level. This is contrary to general planting instructions, but in this case it will allow extra roots to form, giving you a stronger plant. Pack the remainder of the soil in the hole and allow for some settling. Add 3-4 litres of water to drive out air pockets and settle the soil. Once the plant has put on some growth, a layer of mulch or home compost can be added to hold moisture and feed the vine.

Clematis vines, unlike other climbers, do not twist around their support like a honeysuckle or put out hold fast roots like an ivy. They have a leaf stem that wraps around anything that is less than about 2 cm in diameter. Hence, downspouts, 2x4 railings or 4x4 posts will not support vines. To reduce the need for a fancy and visible trellis on the house wall, I have found that heavy fishing line, weed eater cord or light galvanized wire works very well. Drive a 2x2 stake in the ground a few cm from the house, then screw eye hooks into the top of the stake and the soffit under the eaves at the roof. Tie a line to the top hook and then tie knots in the line about every 30 cm before tying it to the bottom hook. The knots will keep the vine from slipping down the line once the plant starts to grow and bloom. The line must not touch the house because the clematis leaf has to wrap around behind the line to hold itself. The offset also allows air movement between the plant and the house.

The line can be redirected horizontally along fences or deck railings as long as the line is away from walls and surfaces. If the vine is cut down during the winter, the only thing showing is a single, almost invisible line. Should you wish to paint the house during the summer when the plant is in full bloom, the upper hook can be removed and the entire vine laid on the ground until the job is finished.

To achieve a more natural look, clematis can be trained to grow up through a small flowering tree. Use a "Prune Hard" summer hybrid and plant it one to two meters away from the trunk. Guide the plant up to the lower branches with the aid of a bamboo stake and then let it run up through the branches to the sun. A tree that bloomed in the spring will have a crop of clematis flowers during mid summer. In the fall, the vine can be cut down and the dead sections pulled out of the tree.

Clematis that have new shoots growing close to the ground in the spring are very susceptible to slug and snail damage. The slugs chew off the new growth faster than it can grow. If no shoots appear or damage is evident, place some slug bait in a covered trap at the base of the plant.

Wilt is the only disease that seems to bother clematis. Infected plants should be cut to the ground and sprayed with a fungicide. They may recover the following year.

Other Perennial Vines

Before selecting a vine to enhance an area, you should determine the purpose for planting. Are you growing the vine for colour, shade, coverage, privacy, fruit or some combination of these? Is it important to have the vine green all year, or is a deciduous plant more suited to the site? What level of maintenance and pruning are you prepared to accept? Contrary to popular belief, not all vines climb in the same way, and their differences will rule out some vines in some areas.

Vines such as honeysuckle, kiwi and wisteria will wrap themselves around a post or tree as they grow up. The new growth is programmed to swing around until it finds something that it can cling to. The Chinese Wisteria (*Wisteria sinensis*) will swing clockwise whereas the Japanese Wisteria (*Wisteria floribunda*) will go counter clockwise, a useful characteristic for identification. "Wrap around" vines will expand in diameter with age and eventually strangle or crush their support column.

Kiwi or *Actinidia chinensis*, is a large, fast growing vine that requires both male and female plants to produce fruit. The fruit is excellent, but the roots are prone to plug drains and the male vine emits a foul odour at times. *A. kolomikta* rarely grows over four meters and has a pink, cream and green variegated leaf with small fruit. It might be a better choice for most areas.

There are many new hybrid varieties of honeysuckle (*Lonicera*) with a great range of colour. They produce flowers on new wood and need constant pruning to prevent them from becoming too rangy. Do not let them twine around other plants as they tend to strangle support plants.

Trumpet vine or Campsis radicans is a large and rangy vine that does well in hot areas, particularly against a south-facing wall.

Ivy, climbing hydrangea, campsis, akelia and Boston ivy are all examples of vines that support themselves by forming an aerial root or "holdfast" that will stick to any surface with which it comes in contact. The glue-like secretion from a holdfast is not easily removed if the vine is taken down. Another drawback is that these vines will collect dust, dead leaves and moisture, a sure way to create rot or attract carpenter ants.

The third and least damaging type of vine has tendrils or leaf tendrils. Grapes and passionflower plants will send out fine tendrils to attach themselves. A clematis will use the leaf stock as a tendril. Any support system used for tendril vines must be far enough away from the wall to allow the tendril room to swing around behind the support and small enough in diameter for the short tendril stem to encircle it.

Golden hops, or *Humulus lupulus*, are not widely used as a horticultural vine. This deciduous plant that will grow five to seven meters per year can act as a screen or feature plant on a high wall. The yellow-green leaves radiate a lot of light and contrast nicely against darker green foliage. Use filament lines or wires for support. Some people are allergic to the oil emitted from the leaves.

The semi-hardy passionflower, or *Passiflora caerulea*, needs some winter protection to ensure its survival. Mine will put on three or four meters of growth each year but it seems to lack the necessary heat to form blooms regularly. It is also very invasive in a protected area.

A less well known but useful evergreen hold fast vine is *Akebia quinata*, a native of Japan. It will grow to six or eight meters, has leaves with five lobes and small chocolate purple coloured flowers. After a hot summer the blooms will form purple sausage shaped fruit.

Check your garden to see if you have a suitable spot for a low maintenance vine that will complement your garden or cover that new trellis.

The Trellis as a Garden Feature

The trellis is a very old garden feature that is underused in many gardens. There are numerous benefits to be gained by skillfully using some form of trellis. A trellis allows for vertical gardening, thereby giving you much more space, particularly useful in small gardens. The plants on a trellis are raised up to where they have more light and can show off their blooms. This can give more height and interest to relatively flat gardens.

The perception of depth can be created with the skilful use of a trellis. The trellis and surrounding landscape can be designed to provide an optical illusion of greater space. This technique would be useful where you have a small, shallow garden. The depth concept can be further reinforced by using warm colours (red, pink, yellow and gold) up close and cool colours (blue and purple) further back.

From a more practical point of view, the trellis can hide an unsightly feature, such as an old fence or stark wall, or provide greater privacy from the street and the neighbours.

Solid fences often look heavy and may dominate a garden setting, but a trellis creates an open, airy feeling. In the summer when more privacy is required, it is possible to create a verdant backdrop with some fast-growing annual or leafy perennial vines. This screen may be an ideal shelter for a protected growing area.

It is not uncommon in old world gardens to see garden rooms created with a trellis as a divider. Each area is used to feature a different theme or series of plants. In local gardens it is a way of separating front and back gardens, and vegetable gardens from landscaped areas.

For gardeners who want to grow tree or vine fruit, the trellis offers lots of options. Fruit trees can be espaliered on wire or wooden trellises. The trees take up less room and can double as a fence or screen. Blackberries and other rambling vines can be trained and made more productive on trellises.

Patios and balconies can sometimes become too hot for mid-day use. You may not be serving retsina and souvlakia for lunch, but you can borrow the Greek-style horizontal trellis with a grape vine for some shade. Grapes are ideal because they leaf out in April and die back in October.

Don't think that all trellises need vines planted at their base. Begonia and fuchsia growers have long used simple beam-type trellises to suspend their hanging baskets.

The most common trellis is the 4'x8' "diamond" or "square" style fence panel but this should not limit your thinking or creativity. A trellis can consist of a single post or pole that will support a climbing rose, or a whole series of pillars with horizontal crosspieces on the tops. Two rows of posts with a connecting trellis roof form an arbour.

To create an invisible trellis on a fence or house wall, use long shank eyehooks and wire or fish line. Vertical wires or lines should have knots every 20 or 30 cm to keep the vines from sliding. For plants that are prone to stick to the cladding on the house, consider using a wooden frame trellis mounted with spaces to keep it 8-10 cm from the wall. This will allow air movement and drying, and will keep the roots off the wall.

A simple trellis-type fence can be enhanced by incorporating an arched gate as part of the plan. There are an endless number of possibilities for trellis arches, such as rectangular, semicircle or Gothic arch patterns.

Although a trellis is lighter and more open than a traditional fence or wall, it must be well secured when installed. On balconies, trellis panels are subjected to wind forces and have the potential to do damage should they blow over. All trellises must be built or installed securely but, ideally, still be removable to allow easy painting, cleaning and renewal.

Look around your garden and see if some form of trellis might improve your garden design or ability to grow a greater variety of plants.

CHAPTER NINETEEN

Trees

Tree Roots

We marvel at the extensive framework of branches and leaves on a large tree but tend to forget there is an equal-sized network of roots under the ground. Most gardeners will judge the health of a tree by its appearance and growing conditions above ground, and ignore what is happening below.

From the time a plant's first roots form from a seed or vegetative cutting, they are affected by gravity. It is thought that the extra growth hormones found in the root tip makes it susceptible to gravitational pull. Roots with severed tips seem to temporarily lose their ability to grow down. Other studies have found that some roots may grow down to get away from cosmic radiation or a part of the light spectrum that we can't see. Some trees, such as arbutus, develop long taproots while others, such as flowering cherries, prefer to grow their roots on the surface. The growth pattern of a tree root is important to know when planting new specimens.

The root cells in various trees seem to be adapted to certain growing conditions and will not tolerate a sudden change. Trees with shallow roots will often die if several feet of new soil (fill) is placed over them. The same thing can happen to other trees if large amounts of soil are removed, or if the roots are covered with blacktop or concrete. Severing large roots on trees may cause the tree to die or be destabilized. Running heavy equipment over the root area and compacting the soil can also cause serious damage to established trees.

Root colour varies greatly with age and from plant to plant. Generally, root tips are white and then turn yellow and brown as they age and increase in size. Black roots usually mean the root is dead, but there are exceptions.

It has been estimated that a very large mature oak tree will have as many as 500 million root tips as part of the root structure below ground. On a warm day these root tips have the ability to draw 400 to 500 litres of water from the ground and pump them into the atmosphere. The evaporation of this water creates a very significant cooling effect on the surrounding environment.

Mixed with this large volume of water being absorbed by the roots are the nutrients that the tree needs to sustain itself and develop new growth. When a tree's top growth is severely pruned, the roots still produce water and nutrients well beyond the tree's new needs which encourages the tree to produce an abundance of new growth. Suckers, water sprouts and rank top growth are typical of excess root capacity.

There is more going on in the subterranean world of tree roots than we once imagined. Most trees have one or more types of root fungus that they rely on to help them extract nutrients from the soil. The fungus, for the most part, have developed a symbiotic relationship with the trees. They are called mycorrhiza (fungus root) and can send out 300 cm of fungal threads for every centimetre of root that is colonized. The fungal threads are very efficient at bringing nutrients and moisture back to the root.

One form of mycorrhiza that infects leguminous plants has the ability to convert nitrogen from the air into plant food. This is why farmers often plant peas or clover as part of a crop rotation pattern.

Recently, plant scientists have discovered that one fungus can infect two different trees, thereby, linking their two "plumbing" systems. They discovered this connection by planting Douglas Fir and White Birch trees close together and then enclosing them in separate greenhouses. By injecting different forms of carbon dioxide and then testing the tissue of each plant, they found the different carbon atoms had been exchanged. Further study showed that the leafy Birch helped the Fir in the summer time when there was heavy shade and the Fir helped the Birch when its leaves had fallen and the Fir was in full light. The mycorrhizae seem to act as the traffic cops, directing the flow of nutrients.

The micorrhizae that infect the roots of salal, huckleberries and blueberries have been found to be hostile to fir trees rather than symbiotic. Having the right combination of plants and micorrhizae provides disease resistance and the best growth opportunity.

Maintaining a healthy soil and the proper conditions for the growth of both micorrhizae and trees will give the best results.

Adding Trees to Your Garden

I am often asked the question, "When is the best time to transplant a large shrub, or plant a new tree?" With so many microclimates and wide fluctuations in the weather from year to year, it is difficult to give specific dates. The best answer I can give is to observe your own environment and watch for the Vine Maple or Japanese Maple leaves to fall. When the leaves are down, it is safe to move almost any shrub or tree. In the fall the soil is still relatively warm and your new tree will start to put on some new root growth, giving it a head start for the beginning of the spring growing season.

The right tree in a small garden gives both scale and balance and provides a focal point to the design, around which other plants can be added. Planting the wrong tree can be a costly mistake if it has to be cut down after a few years because it has become too large or unsuitable for the site.

Choose a tree that has an interesting shape or form and one that is not going to be too big at maturity for the space available. Decide if you want an evergreen or deciduous variety. Evergreens are great for privacy but most deciduous trees tend to be better bloomers and provide more interest throughout the year. They produce vibrant new apple green leaves in the spring, shade in the summer, colourful leaves in the fall and possibly an intricate branch structure for a snow display in the winter.

Trees that are disease resistant and require minimum maintenance are good choices. Native dogwoods and some of the ornamental apples and cherries are lovely trees but are far too prone to disease in damp climates.

At various times during the year you can buy trees grown in pots or field grown trees that have been dug with their root ball wrapped and tied in burlap (B & B or ball and burlap). Young trees in pots are generally sold by height, whereas the more mature field grown trees are sold by caliper (diameter of trunk). The price goes up exponentially as the tree increases in height or the trunk in diameter.

Give considerable thought to the location before planting your tree. Then, dig a hole twice as large as the root ball, removing all large roots and rocks. Mix the soil from the hole with compost on a two to one ratio and place enough of the new mix back in the hole to create a mound that will raise the top of the root ball to be flush with or slightly above the ground. Holding the trunk in an upright position, fill the rest of the hole with the new mix, tamping as you proceed.

Trees that are more than two metres high should be staked and secured for the first two years until their roots become well established. Using two sharpened 2x2 stakes, pound one in on each side of the root ball, being careful not to skewer the roots. Tie the tree trunk to the stakes using belting, fabric or old hose. Make sure the trunk has a little bit of freedom to move as it would in nature. DO NOT use wire to secure the tree as wire is prone to cut the bark or choke the tree. Make sure you check the ties for tightness several times a year, until they are removed.

Water the newly planted tree to drive out excess air in the soil mix and bring the soil into contact with the roots. An organic mulch at the base will finish the job.

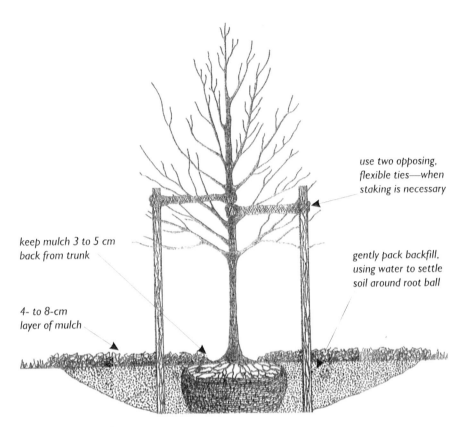

use two opposing,
flexible ties—when
staking is necessary

keep mulch 3 to 5 cm
back from trunk

gently pack backfill,
using water to settle
soil around root ball

4- to 8-cm
layer of mulch

Planting plan for trees.

Here are the names of a few trees that would be suitable for home gardens.

- **Paper Bark Maple** (*Acer griseum*) has very distinctive red peeling bark and great fall colour.

- **Japanese Maples** (*Acer palmatum*) come in more than two dozen different forms and sizes. The leaf colour varies in the summer but all have good fall colour. Some varieties have coloured bark that gives winter interest.

- **Silk Tree** (*Albizia julibrissen*) is slow to leaf out in the spring but is a fast grower. The pink tassel blooms come in August and September when many gardens are at their best.

- **Korean Dogwood** (*Cornus kousa*) has large white blooms that fade to pink with large red strawberry-like fruit and coloured leaves in the fall. It is not as susceptible to disease as our native dogwood. "Satomi" is a pink form.

- **Willow Cotoneaster** (*Cotoneaster salicifolia*) is an evergreen tree that produces a flush of white flowers in the spring and a great show of red berries all winter.

- **Star Magnolia** (*Magnolia stellata*) is one of the best of the species for a small garden. It produces an abundance of small white blooms each spring.

- **Sourwood** (*Oxydendrum arboreum*) produces clusters of lily-of-the-valley type flowers during the summer and has attractive fall colour.

- **Golden Locust** (*Robinia pseudoacacia* 'Frisia') can get to be a fairly large tree but the yellow green leaves against a dark green backdrop can be spectacular all summer.

- **Stewartia** (*Stewartia pseudocamellia*) has year round interest with large white blooms in the Spring, great fall colour and peeling bark and branch structure for the winter.

- **Snow Bell Tree** (*Styrax japonica* or *S. obassia*) is another of the best small trees for home gardens. The pink or white flowers are produced all along the branches in May.

Tree and Shrub Bark

Flowers and foliage provide an abundance of colour and beauty in our gardens for most of the year. Bark and plant structure can also provide interest in the garden when the leaves and flowers

Cornus kousa 'Satomi,' an excellent medium-sized tree.

have fallen away to reveal the inner beauty and colour of a plant. Some tree species stand out when it comes to colourful or patterned bark. They can catch your eye during the dull days of winter.

Maples or the *Acer* family, have a number of varieties with unique bark. *Acer davidi*, *A. grosseri* and *A. capillipes* are all called Snake Bark Maples and have a distinctive lined bark. *A. pensylvanicum* is similar but has more pronounced white lines on dark green bark. *A. griseum* is called the Paper Bark Maple and has orangey-brown bark that peels and flakes off, revealing a lighter rich colour below. While not in the maple family, our native *Arbutus menziesi* is also a good example of a tree trunk with several shades of green, orange and brown colour, with peeling bark. There are few trees in the world that can display this rich colour.

Japanese maples are best known for their fall leaf colour but several also display colourful bark and an interesting structure in their trunks. *Acer palmatum* 'Senkaki' or Coral Bark Maple has a distinctive red bark that gives the tree prominence in the winter. Several of the other *A.palmatum disectum* such as 'Red Laceleaf', 'Crimson Queen' and 'Garnet' will all have gnarled or twisted trunks when they mature, and this can add interest to the winter garden.

There are a half dozen varieties of Birch (*Betula*) with their white bark that will stand out against a dark green backdrop. The best of the species is *B.* 'Jacquemonti' or White Barked Himalayan birch. They are guaranteed to light up a drab yard. If you already have a birch tree and the bark has lost its whiteness, don't be afraid to use some liquid dishwasher detergent, hot water and a scrub brush to remove the algae.

Normally we value the Dogwood (*Cornus*) family for their spring flowers and autumn foliage but there are several specimens that are grown as ground covers and their winter colour. *C. alba* 'Siberica' and *C. sericea* will produce a mass of 1m sucker shoots from the base of the plant, if properly pruned each spring.

The bark on this new wood is a deep red and lights up in the winter sunshine. *C. alba 'Flaviramea'* is a close relative but has yellow bark instead of red. Wood that is two years or older will usually lose its colour and should be cut out.

Prunus serrula is a member of the cherry family and has bark that is very shiny with a rich mahogany colour. As the tree grows, the bark stretches and breaks, causing it to peel in horizontal strips, creating a variegated banding effect. This is certainly a tree that stands out in the winter.

Peeling bark of arbutus (madrona) tree.

Most berry canes stay green or turn brown over the winter but *Rubus cockburnianus* or the Whitewashed Bramble produces long, arching canes that are covered with a white coating that gives them prominence in the winter sunshine. Unfortunately, they do not bear edible fruit.

Scarlet Willow, *Salix alba 'Chermesina'*, and Golden willow, *S. alba 'Vitelina'* both produce sucker shoots that come into view once the leaves are down in the fall.

A Blue Spruce, *Picea pungens*, will look good at anytime of the year but is particularly striking with its frosty blue colour during cold sunny weather in winter. Japanese Cedar or *Cryptomeria japonica* is not widely grown and, unlike most conifers, it turns a purple-brown in the winter and then back to a coppery-green in the summer

Conifers don't generally lose their needles but the Larch family is an exception. As with many bare trees, the intricate branch structure can be striking when the dark bark on each branch is highlighted with a ribbon of pure white snow.

If your landscaping is in need of some additional bushes or trees, think winter and ask yourself what you can add that will brighten up the garden in this off-season.

Tree Care

The problem with living in a temperate rain forest is that trees are numerous and they tend to grow very fast. Most property owners at some time will have to hire an arborist to prune or remove overgrown trees.

Before having any work done, here are a few things to consider. Some companies are run by certified arborists and their crews are well trained. Others may have limited qualifications and lack experience. Talk to friends or neighbours that have had work done and then call at least three companies for quotes. Ask for references or the addresses of some sites where they have done work. Make sure the price given is a firm written quote and not just an estimate. The quote should state clearly what is included: Are the remaining branches to be thinned, pruned or shaped? Will the wood be removed or stacked? Will there be any damage to the understory plants? Will all the debris be cleaned up and removed? The lowest price is not always the best deal.

The company you engage to do the work should have at least $3 million in liability insurance and be covered by the WCB. For work that is close to hydro (electricity) lines, the company will need a permit and a crew that is properly qualified by BC Hydro to do the work. Depending on which municipality you live in, you may also need a special permit to remove trees of a certain size, trees close to a stream bed or those on steep slopes. It would be wise to contact the local municipal government arborist for specific details.

Removing large trees often has an impact on the neighbours and they might appreciate knowing what you plan to do, particularly if some branches are likely to fall into their yard or you need access for debris removal. Chain saws and chippers are extremely noisy and most people would choose to be absent if they know when the work is to be done.

Cutting trees on your own property is generally not a problem, but knowing the location of your property line may be. Cutting a tree and then finding out that it is not on your property can be extremely expensive. Some property owners have been sued for cutting trees on private property or municipal parkland. Do not rely on the tree company for advice if there is any doubt that the tree is on your property.

Timing is not important when it comes to removing trees, but it can be for pruning or thinning. Coniferous trees can be worked on almost any time during the year, but one has to be more selective with deciduous trees. Broadleaf or deciduous trees start their burst of new growth in the spring allowing the tree to fill out and regenerate a reasonable amount of new growth within a few months. This is particularly true for laurel hedges that have to be cut back to bare wood. Other trees, such as maple and birch, generate a heavy flow of sap in the spring and are prone to bleed if cut at the wrong time. Bleeding will not kill the tree but robs it of some energy and may make it more prone to disease. Some trees are best left until the spring growth is over before cutting, to avoid excess growth of suckers and water shoots.

The practice of topping large coniferous trees is almost a thing of the past because it creates top-heavy trees that are likely to be a problem in the future. The procedure now is to spiral prune the branches in order to let in more light, reduce the wind drag, and create windows in the tree for a view. Removing the lower branches can improve the light conditions, open up the view, and show off the massive trunks typical of west coast coniferous trees.

Douglas Fir and Red Cedar are generally well-rooted trees and are not as prone to blow over as the Western Hemlock. Hemlocks are far more disease-prone and can snap off if there is a weak point in the trunk.

There is a definite ratio between the root structure of a tree and the top growth. When this ratio is disrupted by pruning, thinning or topping, the tree will be stimulated to grow rapidly and re-establish this natural ratio. Tree work is seldom a "one time" project.

Bamboo

The mention of bamboo will generate a strong negative reaction from many gardeners. I used to feel the same way, after having spent many hours grubbing out an unwanted and out of control thicket of bamboo that a former homeowner had planted. Over the years I have come to appreciate the many species of bamboo as attractive landscaping plants, providing they are grown in the right place. Bamboo will give your garden a distinctive tropical look.

More than a thousand species are referred to as bamboo, but only a small number of them are actually classified as true *Bambusa* which is the Latin form of the Malaysian name. The American Bamboo Society (ABS) source list has 383 different species, sub-species, varieties, forms, cultivars and clones. Unfortunately, plant taxonomists can't agree on names and some varieties have three or four different Latin names as well as several common names.

Most species come from Southeast Asia, but a few can be found in America and Africa. The tropical world has the majority of species, but bamboo also grows in the sub-tropics and north into temperate climates. Some bamboo species are hardy to Zone 5 if well mulched. Full sun is preferred by most species but some will grow well in the shade.

Bamboo is technically a member of the grass family but differs greatly in size. It ranges from 5 cm (2") to more than 35 m (100') in height for the large timber bamboo. The largest hardy bamboo is *Phyllostachys heterocycla* which can reach 20 m and form a 18 cm diameter culm or stalk. It is widely grown in China where it is used for plywood, paper, and flooring, and in place of piping for scaffolding. The young tender shoots can grow from 5 cm to 1 m per day and can be served as food or fed to animals as fodder. Panda bears live exclusively on bamboo shoots and leaves, and find them to be very nutritious.

Unlike grass, bamboo is programmed to flower once every 10 to 120 years depending on the species. Plants derived from a single source will all bloom the same year. This happened in Vancouver with our common *Phyllostachys bambusoides* in 1972. Surprisingly, most species die after they bloom.

Before you purchase bamboo, check on its growth pattern. Clumping plants will spread 2 to 4 cm per year, moderate spreading plants will spread 30 to 60 cm per year, and running plants will travel 1.5 to 5 m per year. Maximum height is also a factor to consider. Dwarf bamboo will grow 5 cm to 1 m, small 1 to 5 m, mid-size 5 to 12 m and timber 12 to 35 m. The culm or stalk will vary in proportion to the height. Many species have distinct culm and leaf colorations.

Separating a section of bamboo from the mother plant can be done in two different ways. A small section of rhizome with one or two clumps about a metre high can be cut from the outside of a plant. It will take several years to develop a good-sized plant from this type of cutting. The other option is to remove a larger block of rhizomes with up to a dozen or more clumps. A sharp axe or saw will be necessary to separate the tough rhizomes.

Look to buy commercial plants that are pot bound to the point of breaking the pot. This will allow them to expand rapidly as soon as they are planted in the ground.

Bamboo rhizomes can be controlled from spreading in any one of three ways: annual root pruning, a concrete foundation, or a bamboo barrier. A barrier made from 30 to 40 mil polyurethane that is at least 60 cm deep will contain the spread of bamboo. A suitable root run or bed for timber bamboo would be 9 sq. m, for mid-sized plants 3 sq. m and for small plants 1 sq. m.

Taking care of bamboo is relatively simple. Feed with a slow release lawn fertilizer and keep it watered all year round, but not to the point of having wet feet. Keep the rhizomes well mulched in the winter, as they will not tolerate frost. Potted plants can be moved to a frost-free area or sunk in the ground. Tying a clump of culms together will give greater winter protection. Prune out the older clumps in the early spring to renew the stand.

Most species of bamboo are relatively disease free but they can be infected with mealy bugs, aphids, mites and scale. Use an appropriate insecticide or try a very light horticultural oil in the spring. As a last resort, you can always shave the plant to the ground and start over again with new culms.

Getting rid of existing bamboo can be a problem. Use several applications of Roundup, both spring and fall, or keep the culms shaved to the ground for three consecutive years. You may need a digging machine to remove a large mass of rhizomes.

Hedges

As a garden feature, the hedge goes back to Greek and Roman times and has been important in gardens ever since.

Different societies have used the hedge for different purposes. After castles became obsolete, many Europeans tried to emulate fortress walls by growing large hedges. The French under Louis XIV lined their estate avenues with trees that were shaped to form enormous hedges. In the low exposed coastal areas of Holland, hedges provided the only available protection from the constant wind. To add interest to the common hedges, some Dutch gardeners began clipping them into unique shapes and forms that developed into the practice of topiary.

Formal European estate gardens used low neatly-trimmed hedges to create complex geometric patterns, symbolic knots, or to define and outline flower beds and gravel horse paths. The gardens were often so large that the nobility would go for a ride in the garden rather than a walk.

Where enclosure or protection was required and building materials like stone and wood were in short supply, growing a hedge, and in particular a thorn hedge, became a viable alternative to a fence or wall. In some cases, the addition of a deep ditch or rock berm enhanced the barrier, a fact the Canadian Tank Corp became painfully aware of in Normandy during World War II.

Today, hedges are used for privacy or as a backdrop for colourful flowers and shrubs. High hedges can form the "walls" of a garden enclosure, creating a special setting. With protection on all four sides, the walled garden can have a distinct microclimate.

Hedge plants come in many forms. They can be divided into: conifers, broadleaf evergreens and deciduous. Some conifers respond better than others and traditionally yew (*Taxus*) has been used more than any other tree for hedging. Pyrmidal cedars are currently very popular. Native hemlocks (*Tsuga*) and cedar (*Thuja*) are commonly used here in the Pacific Northwest.

The most common broadleaf evergreen used for hedging is boxwood (*Buxus*) followed by laurel (*Prunus*) and holly (*Ilex*). Deciduous hedges are less common today because they lose their colour in the winter.

Planning a new hedge is important because if you make a mistake, the problem will be with you for a long time. Make your choice of a plant with consideration for appearance, hardiness, longevity and maintenance. Fast-growing plants may fill in quickly but frequent shearing to maintain a manageable height may be a major problem. Know the potential diameter of the plants and spacing distance, otherwise you may have gaps in the hedge for years. This is particularly true for the pyramidal cedars that should be spaced on 60 cm (2') centres or less.

Digging a wide planting trench and breaking up the native soils will help encourage the spread of roots. Additional topsoil should be used if the native soil is too poor or shallow. Bone meal or slow release fertilizer can be added to give the plants additional food.

Hedge maintenance is critical once the hedge has been

planted. Start pruning and shaping the plants as soon as they show significant growth. This will cause them to bush and fill out. The less ladder work required when clipping a hedge, the easier the job will be. Do not let the hedge get too wide as this makes the centre area at the top difficult to reach from either side. If you want a 2 m (6') hedge, initially prune the hedge to 1 2/3 m (5') and let it slowly grow up to the higher level. Once some hedges get to the desired height they cannot be stopped permanently at that height or pruned back to a lower level.

Most coniferous hedges, unlike the broadleaf types, will not form new growth on old brown stems. It is essential to leave 3 to 5 cm (1-2") of green growth on the surface of the hedge or it will be permanently ruined. Don't let an amateur or poorly-trained gardener touch a coniferous hedge unless you are sure they know what they are doing.

Broadleaf evergreen and deciduous hedges can generally be cut back hard every few years when they become too tall or overgrown. The best time to do this is in the early spring just as the new growth begins to appear. When doing major pruning, be

Coniferous (Red Cedar) hedge pruned into brown wood.

sure to cut both sides and the top, or much of the new growth will be on the uncut surface only.

Regular shearing can be done almost anytime, except in mid summer and mid winter. The ideal time is after the main flush of growth has finished in the late spring or early summer. Mid to late fall sheerings should be done very lightly.

CHAPTER TWENTY

Propagation

Propagation Methods

Gardeners generally take great delight in being able to pass on plants to others who share their love of gardening. I rarely visit a garden where I am not offered a cutting or seedling of a plant in which I have shown an interest. If you want to propagate plants to give to friends or for yourself, here are a few simple techniques.

There are two main ways plants reproduce. Sexual reproduction is carried out by seeds and spores. Asexual reproduction relies on a plant's ability to send out new roots and a growing stem from some part of the old root, stem or leaf. This method of plant propagation is generally much faster and easier. In fact, it is the only way to propagate plants such as bananas, pineapples and navel oranges that don't normally produce seed. Some of the most common propagation techniques are as follows.

- **Natural suckering** for chaenomales, raspberries, sumac and hardy fuchsia. The natural sucker or root sucker at the side of the root ball can be cut off and replanted during the dormant season.

- **Root cutting** for primulas, poppies, phlox, romneya, clerodendrum, paulownia and campsis. Whole plants or sections of roots can be lifted and the root cut into sections and replanted to produce new plants. Some plants such as kiwi and morninglory are hard to kill because the roots are so good at growing from root cuttings.

- **Tubers and tuberous roots** for potatoes, begonias and dahlias. As long as you have a section of swollen root and an eye, a new plant can be generated. Dahlia cuttings also work very well for rapid propagation.

- **Rhizomes** for calla and canna lilies, iris, strelitzia, lily of the valley, peonies and rhubarb. The rhizomes can be lifted after flowering, washed, cut into sections and the wounds left to dry briefly before replanting.

- **Natural division** is for bulbs such as daffodils and tulips. Lilies can be propagated by offsets at the base of the flowering stem, bulbils that grow in the leaf axil or bulb scaling where the separate scales on a bulb are peeled off and grown into new bulbs. Bulb scoring is used for hyacinth or other tunicate bulbs where the base or root structure of the bulb is scored at right angles and then placed in a well ventilated area to allow new bulblets to grow from the base of the old bulb.

- **Simple division** for most herbaceous perennials with fibrous roots as well as hardy fuchsia and hydrangea. As a perennial becomes too large and the centre section of the plant becomes old, woody and susceptible to disease it will benefit from dividing. The new outer sections of the root ball can be replanted or given away.

- **Offsets and runners** for crassula, sempervivum, ajuga, saxifragia, strawberries and tolmea. If left, the offsets and runners will take root on their own, but to speed up the process they can be cut off and planted where required.

- **Layering or tip layering** for most common woody flowering shrubs and vine berry bushes. This is the easiest way to root rhododendrons. Low-level branches can be pinned down so they are partially covered by soil. The section of branch under the soil should have an angle cut about a third of the way through and the cut held open by a small pebble or matchstick. Once the branch has rooted after a season's growth, the new plant can be cut free and potted up.

- **Air Layering** is more commonly used for houseplants but can also work with shrubs. The stem is partially cut, as in layering, and then padded with damp sphagnum moss and wrapped with plastic, allowing the roots to form in the moss before the new plant is cut free. A similar method can be used on rhododendrons by running a cut branch through a notched 1 gallon pot full of soil set up on a stake or post. When the branch roots and is cut free you already have a new potted plant. Some garden shops now sell a specialized pot for this purpose.

- **Stooling and dropping** for japonica, lilacs, callunas, daboecia, ericas, hebes and vaccinium. These plants will respond to rooting when their crowns are buried in several centimetres of soil, allowing each branch to become a new plant. The branches can be arranged in a row or spread out in a circle.

As a general rule all root cutting should be done during the dormant period and any plants covered with soil take a growing season to produce a new root structure.

Seeds and Seeding

Planting seeds is a relatively easy task, if you observe a few basic rules. To plant varieties that are slow to develop or large numbers of seeds, you need a greenhouse. For a few annuals, perennials or vegetable seeds, such as tomatoes or zucchini, a fluorescent light or a south-facing window will do.

Not all seeds are ideal for windowsill growing. Check the back of the package or ask a experienced grower how tolerant the seeds are when it comes to germination temperatures, planting methods or rates of growth. Seeds that require very precise germination temperature or seedlings which take a long time to mature should be avoided.

Many English garden books use the term "seed compost" to describe a medium for germinating seeds. This, however, is a misnomer because most soil and compost, as we know it, contains too many types of fungus which can kill seedlings. The best material to use is a sterile peat product such as Mica-Peat or Reddi Earth. With limited space it is best to plant the seeds in 8cm x 12cm plastic trays and then transplant into small pots as required. Be sure to sterilize the trays in a weak bleach solution before planting.

Some seeds need light to germinate and should be planted on the surface. When in doubt plant some above and some below to find out which works best. Seed trays are best watered from the bottom with lukewarm water and covered with clear plastic wrap to retain the moisture. A 25 watt light bulb or other small heat source provides bottom heat and will help maintain a constant temperature. A small thermometer will allow you to determine the exact temperature for germination. Remove the seed tray from the heat source as soon as the plants break through the soil.

Seedlings, once they have formed their first true leaves, are ready to be transplanted into trays or 6cm pots and proper potting soil. Be careful not to damage the stems or roots of the little seedlings and cover them temporarily with a loose fitting plastic wrap to get them over the shock of transplanting. Seedlings generally grow stronger and bushier if the temperature is reduced soon after they are transplanted. Apply a weak solution of transplant fertilizer to the base of the tray or pot.

Heirloom Seeds

With all the concern about genetically modified food and the push by multinational seed companies to introduce patented hybrid varieties, more gardeners are rediscovering the old varieties of flowers and vegetables grown by their grandparents. Other gardeners are interested in heirloom seeds because of their unique characteristics and diversity, or because they wish to help preserve the gene pool within a species.

Plant breeders have produced some exceptional new plants in recent years but not all of them are well suited to the needs of backyard gardeners. Many hybrid plants will not come true from saved seed the following year. This forces gardeners to buy new, expensive seed each year.

Heirloom seeds, on the other hand, have been grown and selected for their performance over hundreds of years. Many of these seeds came with immigrant families from other countries and have been passed down from generation to generation.

Heirloom seeds would not have survived if they had not met the needs of gardeners in relation to flavour, colour, scent, productivity and disease resistance. Too often it seems new vegetable varieties are developed with an emphasis on shelf life, productivity and appearance, rather than flavour and nutrition.

Many old-fashioned plant varieties have stood the test of time when it comes to disease, thus needing fewer pesticides or fungicides to protect them. If they were highly susceptible to disease or pests, they would not have survived.

Maintaining a wide genetic diversity in plants has become

more important as we see more and more hybridization being done using the same parent plants. The recent problem affecting commercial banana plantations all over the world is a good example. Virtually all commercial bananas have been cloned from one species that is susceptible to a deadly black fungus. The fungus disease is spreading rapidly, killing banana plants throughout the banana-producing countries which will, no doubt, have a major impact on both price and availability of bananas in the future.

Over the last two decades many heirloom seed companies have sprung up to fill the demand created by home gardeners who want something other than the new hybrids. Recently, I was looking through the Baker Creek Heirloom Seed catalogue and was surprised to see such a wide variety of seeds, so many of them unique.

There are red and white ringed beets, purple cauliflower, a dozen types of ornamental corn, and 27 varieties of snow peas. I have seen several different kinds of eggplant but had no idea there at least 30 varieties grown around the world. They come in every imaginable size, shape and colour.

Melons are not widely grown in our cool climate but greenhouse owners might be interested in some of the 50 varieties of melons, not including watermelons.

The list of radishes includes red, white, black and green with sizes up to 60 cm long and 8 cm in diameter along with a half dozen 19th-century turnip varieties.

The squash and tomato varieties are too numerous to count and come in every size, shape and colour.

If you want to try your hand at grinding your own flour, they even have seeds for Red Turkey wheat, a popular bread-making wheat from the 1800's.

For more information you can check an heirloom seed website at www.rareseeds.com.

CHAPTER TWENTY-ONE

Tips for the Gardener

These helpful tips and activities are things that I have found useful over the years. Some are mentioned elsewhere in the book and will act as reminders. I am sure you have some of your own ideas that you can add to the list.

1. Prevent broken tomato stems by pre-tying strings on tomato stakes at one-foot intervals. When you see a tomato plant that needs tying, the string is already there to secure the plant.

2. Tomatoes grown in the greenhouse can be trained on a single string attached to the roof or rafter. Twist the stem of the tomato around the string as it continues to grow, locking each leaf behind the string.

3. Short of space for cucumbers and squash? Train them to grow up on a wire hoop or fence. As large squash form they can be supported with a nylon-stocking hammock.

4. Four-litre bleach containers cut at a 45-degree angle make great scoops for soil, peat and ashes. Cut away the top quarter of a bleach jug, saving the handle section and make a fertilizer or lime container that won't fall over or become damp on the bottom.

5. 35mm film canisters make excellent seed containers. Label the top with masking tape and store in a cool site. Ask for them at a photo shop.

6. Prevent soil compaction in the garden by laying down old cedar fence boards between the rows of plants. The boards take the weight of the wheelbarrow, keep your shoes from getting muddy, and act as a natural slug trap.

7. Discarded fishnet hung on permanent hooks along a fence or shed makes an excellent temporary support for beans, peas or sweet peas.

8. To keep sword and deer ferns attractive, they should be cut to the ground in the early spring each year. The fronds will not break down in the compost but make a great mulch when ground up with a lawn mower.

9. Dried cow patties soaked overnight in a pail of water make a rich manure tea or liquid fertilizer.

10. Cut triangular holes at the base of a can and then add slug bait to the can. Place a lid on the top of the can to keep it dry and prevent dogs, cats, birds and kids from coming into contact with the poison.

11. Partially-decayed or old compost piles are a great place to plant vegetables. Cucumbers, squash, tomatoes, potatoes and corn will all grow well from the sides or top of the pile.

12. Try growing parsnips in a cone shaped hole filled with compost-enriched soil. The small roots will feed on the compost and fill the cone shaped hole with large well-formed parsnips.

13. Parsnips are slow to germinate and break through the soil surface. Planting quick-growing radishes in the same spot will not only help the parsnips emerge but will provide a second vegetable crop.

14. Try covering your raised beds with clear plastic for the winter. A slight camber on the bed will improve the drainage and prevent leaching. Early spring sunshine will germinate weed seeds so they should be removed before regular planting takes place.

15. Warming the soil with a mini greenhouse will help almost any type of seed germinate more quickly in the early spring. Lay two 2x4 boards six inches apart and cover with clear plastic to create a 2x6 inch air space that will heat and warm the soil and seeds below.

16. Cutworms (caterpillars) that feed on vegetables, such as tomatoes, return to the soil each day and can be found at the junction between the firm, wet soil and the loose, dry soil. Cultivate a six to eight inch diameter circle around the base of the plant and you are sure to find the culprit without having to use insecticide.

17. Tomatoes that suffer from blossom end rot (grey spot at the base) do not have a disease but are usually showing signs of calcium or magnesium deficiency or frequent droughts.

18. Tomatoes that form properly but fail to ripen properly on their shoulders are suffering from a lack of potassium (potash).

19. Some flower and vegetable seeds need soil temperatures of 14° to 16°C to germinate. Early spring temperatures will cause them to rot unless they are pre-germinated in a flat in

the house or greenhouse. Pre-germinate beans, cabbage, corn, peas and tomatoes.

20. To provide more space for seedlings in the greenhouse during the spring growing season, add an extra shelf by suspending it from the rafters on old blind cords.

21. Check your local venetian blind store for leftover slats. They come in a variety of colours, are UV treated, and make excellent plant labels.

22. Early plantings can be protected from chilling winds by using three or four stakes to support a bottomless bag over a plant. Cleaner's plastic bags work well for larger plants or a group of plants.

23. Gardeners who have run out of space should consider more vertical gardening. Fences, walls, netting and trellises can add up to 50% more growing space.

24. Trimming the lower branches on shrubs such as rhododendrons generally make more work for the gardener. The dense root structure is not a good growing area and letting in the light creates more space for weeds. Branches close to the ground spring back after mowing reducing the need for edging. Grow your flowers out in front of the shrubs.

25. Bulb leaves should show several inches of yellow on the ends before they are cut off. NEVER tie the leaves of bulbs.

26. Small bulbs such as crocus and snowdrops are best planted near the sidewalk or the edge of the bed. Not only are they more visible but the leaves can be flipped out of the bed

when planting annuals and then back in when waiting for them to mature.

27. A short two- or three-metre section of a dead bushy deciduous shrub or tree driven into the ground makes a good support for a fast growing clematis or vine. It can be removed and replaced the following year.

28. Many garden beds will support two tiers of colour. Plant early flowering primula or muscari bulbs under roses or impatiens under tall fuchsia standards.

29. A soil screen hung by two loops of rope from an overhead branch or support is a good way to clean rock from garden soil. Borrow your neighbour's wheelbarrow so you have one for hauling and one under the screen.

30. Two sections of hollow pipe imbedded in the lawn allows for the quick setting up of poles for a badminton or volleyball net. Additional guy strings can be pegged to the lawn with large galvanized spikes.

31. Rail fences made with boards can be converted into plant shelves. Nail a horizontal board on the top rail so it extends out over the west side and another to the lower rail on the east side

INDEX

About the Author

Roy Jonsson started gardening as a child learning at the knee of his father. He spent many an hour learning how to weed long rows of carrots and beets.

After graduating from the University of British Columbia and purchasing his own home he started taking landscaping and horticulture courses. He has been teaching gardening and landscaping for twenty–seven years and is currently an instructor for VanDusen Botanic Garden and for the Continuing Education Department in North Vancouver. In 1990 he was given an Instructor Excellence Award and in 2000 he won the BCLNA Educator of the Year Award.

In addition to his teaching and consulting he has contributed numerous articles to garden publications and written the gardening column "Sow It Grows" in the North Shore News for the past fourteen years. He has been a member of the Garden Writers Association since 2001.

Roy has also worked in the commercial composting industry and has done a number of local and international projects related to composting and horticulture. He belongs to the British Columbia Landscape and Nursery Association and recently served on the Landscape Standard Committee for the development of green roofs.